PHP: The Ultimate

Step by Step guide for beginners on how to learn PHP and MYSQL programming in just 6 hours

By Emily Goldstein

Table of Contents

INTRODUCTION

Are you inspired by the idea of making your own website? Ever thought about how cool is it to have a website that has a log-in/log-out functionality? Need to figure out how to Create, Read, Update or Delete (CRUD) records in a database? Have you lost track of your past instructional exercises? Having considered all these questions, I'm going to show you how to make a website without any outside help where you will know each and every subtle element on how the PHP website code functions. If you are new to back-end web development, this instructional book is for you.

I'll clarify everything in your point of interest so that you won't need to research some specific techniques being used in PHP. To keep things as straightforward as possible, we won't be using any complex systems. Additionally, I won't be concentrating on the websites design because we are after the functionalities. However, it's anything but difficult to execute the design. What this book will be doing is an easy yet exhaustive analysis of the entire PHP Coding process.

So, what is PHP? In the event that you own a site or need a site designed, you may need to know the response to this question. Consider - in 1999 it was assessed there were more than 100,000 sites utilizing PHP to upgrade their own particular site. Today, there are more than 1,000,000 sites utilizing PHP.

PHP is a prevalent and broadly utilized programming dialect utilized for site improvement. PHP stands for PHP: Hypertext Preprocessor.

In the early years of the Internet, most destinations were static content pages. As the Internet advanced, individuals needed sites with more intuitive functionality, for example, visitor books and contact frames. PHP was the ideal instrument and still is today.

PHP is an exceptionally strong and experienced programming dialect. It was initially released in 1995 and has developed to turn into one of the favored dialects for site advancement. It runs on the server side and is exceptionally secure. Now that it's out in the open, most facilitating organizations give PHP their facilitating bundles.

In the event that you require an interactive site, with components like visitor books and contact shapes, you can learn PHP programming yourself, purchase a site bundle, or contract a Professional PHP Programmer. A great number of people don't have room, schedule or capability to take in a programming dialect e.g. PHP and choose to acquire site packs. One recent my recent customers acquired a do-it-without anyone else's help site pack from a vast re-sell. These packs, however offer fundamental sites that can work for a few individuals, have little functionality and offer restricted highlights.

In the wake of battling with it, this customer employed me to develop his site. After finishing it, he now has a site that is lovely and has incredible functionality and interactive elements that his customers need. His site is a long way past what a site pack could have ever given. This is the distinction of PHP!

CHAPTER 1

SETTING UP YOUR SERVER

Since now you have everything set and ready to go, as the nuts and bolts of programming goes, we should begin by making a basic shout out of "hi world" in the server.

To start with, go to the catalog where you introduced your XAMPP (Commonly in C:\xampp). From that point, go to the htdocs envelope (Commonly in C:\xampp\htdocs) and make an organizer named "My-FirstWebsite".

From that part, you have now made a Local URL for your website. That envelope will be utilized to supply in all website records (.html, .php, .css, .js, and so forth.). Open up your content manager and now we can begin!

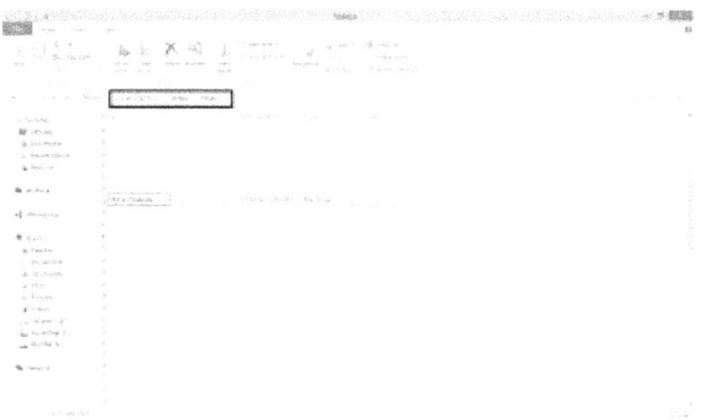

I utilize superb content as my word processor. On the off chance that you're utilizing Notepad++ or any other processors, it's alright. It's not so much of a major component yet because it's only an inclination on which one you might want to utilize.

What we will do is a fundamental HTML page and presentation "hi world" from the server, utilizing an essential PHP language structure. We will then sort the accompanying grammar:

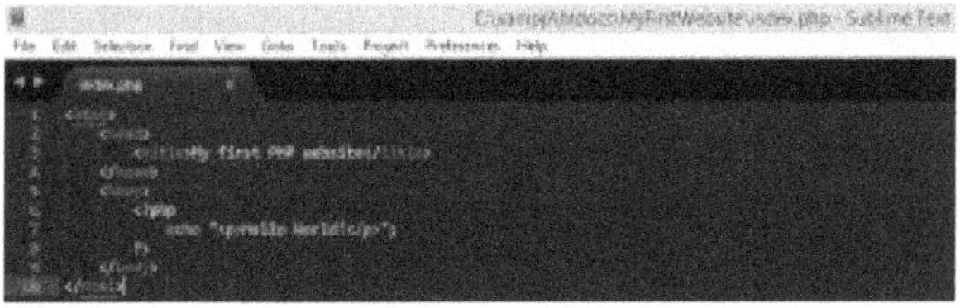

ABOVE CODING:

```
<html>

<head>

<title>My first PHP Website</title>

</head>

<body>

<?php
```

echo “<p>Hello World!</p>”;

?>

</body>

</html>

Save the document to the “MyFirstWebSite” Folder and name it as “index.php”. (Index as seen on the top bar of the picture)

Given that you have the record, we should now open your XAMPP control board. In the event that it doesn’t show up on your desktop, it is situated in your XAMPP envelope as seen on the picture:

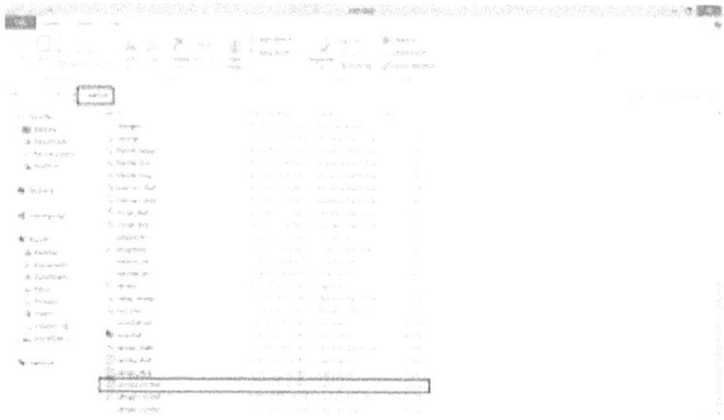

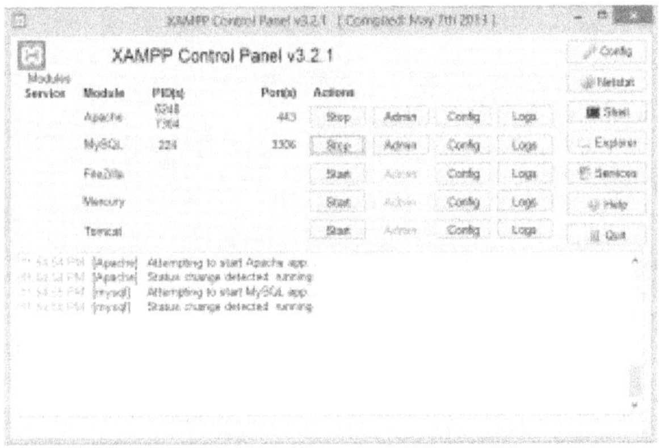

Now that it's there, Run your Apache and mySQL by tapping the "Begin" catch on the activities segment. You ought to see an irregular PID(s) and the default port number. **Apache** is the name of our web server in which it will handle every one of the documents and also serve as the correspondence to the web program and **MySQL** is our database which will store the greater part of our data.

Open up your web program and in the location bar, click localhost. You ought to see the menu of your XAMPP.

On the off chance that it's the first time when you run it, it will ask what dialect you would incline toward, just basically pick one and it will lead you to the menu. On the off chance that you will see the index is localhost/xampp, it's the place the default page drives you regardless of the whether you write in localhost.

On the off chance that you will see that the URL is MyFirstWebsite, it is gotten from the htdocs organizer and it naturally peruses documents that are named "index"(Be it index.html, index.aspx, and so on), which serves as the default page. Nonetheless, writing localhost/MyfirstWebsite/index.php is important. You can also make your custom name for the URL by essentially renaming the organizer but how about we simply stick to MyFirstWebsite for now.

Note: If you don't have a record named list and you enter the URL, you will get a slip 404 for not having the document on the server. In case you do have distinctive documents that are not named index<extention>, you need to determine the particular record name. E.g: localhost/MyfirstWebsite/page.php.

1.1 Creating the public HTML Pages

The next step is that we should change our website and include a registration page where our clients can enroll and also a Log-in page immediately after getting enlisted. We should also adjust our landing page with the accompanying code:

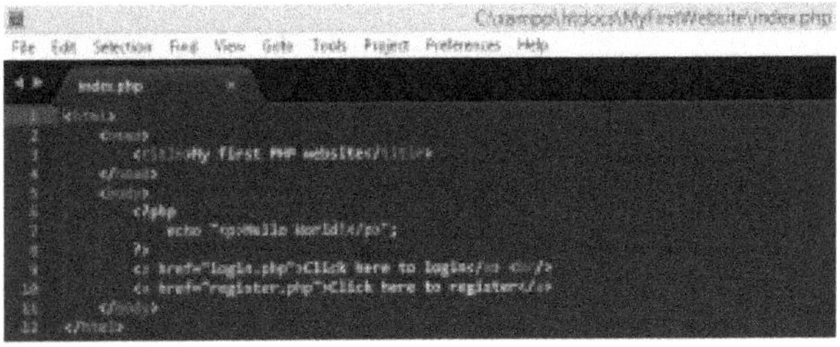

CODE ABOVE:

```
<html>

<head>

<title>My first PHP Website</title>

</head>

<body>
```

```
<?php
echo “<p>Hello World!</p>”;
    ?>
<a href=”login.php”> Click here to login
<a href=”register.php”> Click here to register
</body>
</html>
```

It should be obvious by now that we have just included 2 connections which are for the Login and register. We should make the registration page first. As you can see, it’s only an essential structure where the client can include his/her accreditations. For the login page, insert this code:

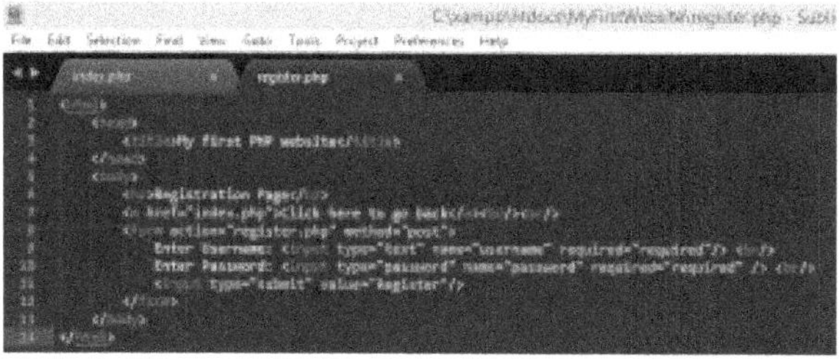

Insight: Just duplicate the same code to make things easier and faster.

login.php

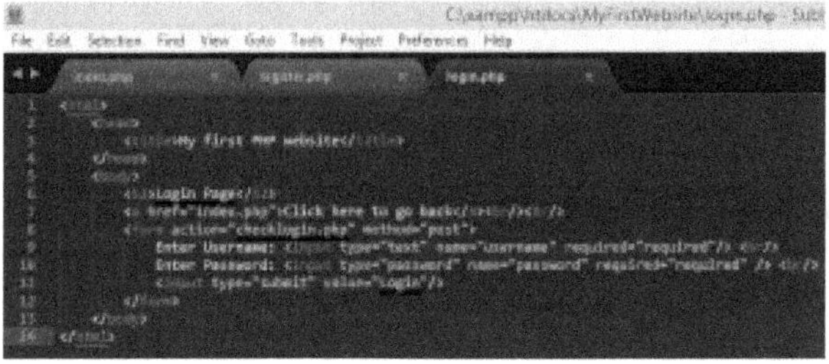

CODE ABOVE:

```
<html>

<head>

<title>My first PHP Website</title>

</head>

<body>

<h2>Login Page</h2>

<a href=”index.php”>Click here to go back<br/><br/>

<form action=”checklogin.php” method=”POST”>

        Enter Username: <input type=”text” name=”username” required=”required” /><br/>
```

```
Enter password: <input type=”password” name=”password” required=”required” /><br/>

<input type=”submit” value=”Login”/>

</form>

</body>

</html>
```

Fundamentally, it’s still the same code as from the register.php but the adjustments/progressions made were the ones underlined.

Try running localhost/MyFirstWebsite again and your pages ought to appear like this:

index.php

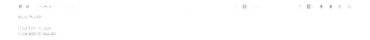

login.php

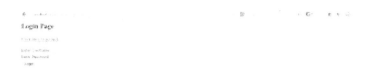

register.php

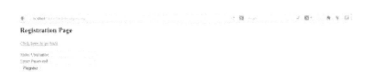

1.2 Creating the database and it's tables

Now that have our most important page for all people in general, how about we continue to the database?

To start with, select localhost/phpmyadmin. This will lead you to the phpmyadmin landing page:

Localhost/phpmyadmin

From that point, go to the Databases tab situated on top then from the content box in the center, select first_db then tap on make. Simply leave the Collation as shown below:

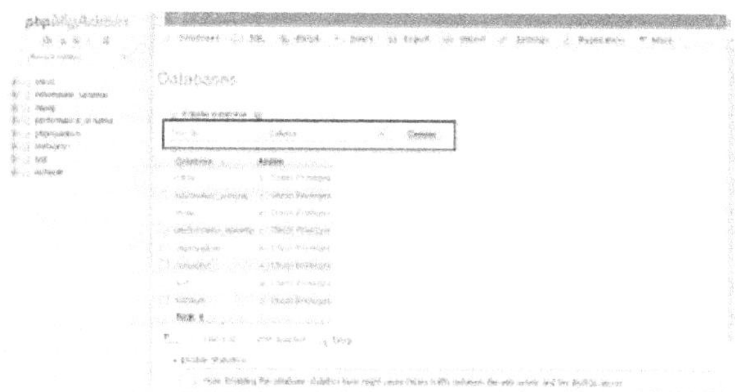

You have now effectively made your first database.

From that point, how about we make a table in which we can enroll our clients and showcase data? To start with, click on first_db situated on the left side and make a table named clients with 3 segments then tap on Go.

For the table's structure, choose to have the accompanying fields then tap on recovery:

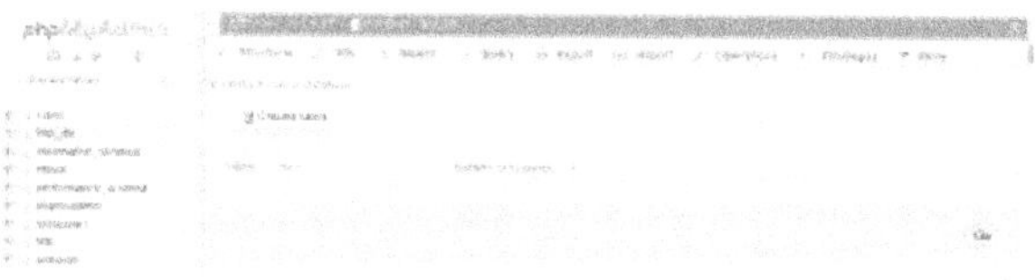

Group: Column Name - Type - Length - Null

Property - Other Properties

Id - INT - N/A - Not Null - Auto Increment

Username - varchar - 50 - Not null

Secret key - varchar - 50 - Not null

Leave everything as default if it is not determined.

Note: You have to sroll to the right of that page for the auto_increment. I simply altered the photo to fit the A_I field

Next, make another table named rundown with 7 sections and for the table's structure:

id - INT - N/A - Not Null - Auto Increment

points of interest - content - Not null

date_posted - varchar - 30 - Not null

time_posted - Time - Not null

date_edited - varchar - 30 - Not null

time_edited - Time - Not null

open - varchar - 5 - Not null

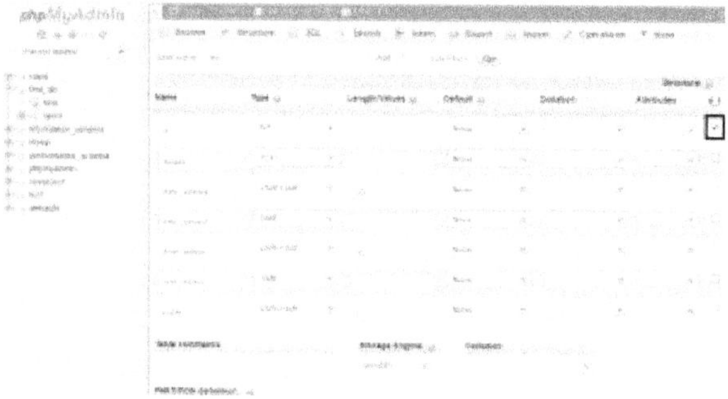

1.3 **Adding users to the database**

Since we have our tables, we should proceed to the fun part, getting your enlistment page usable. From your registration.php, include the html codes add-on below:

register.php

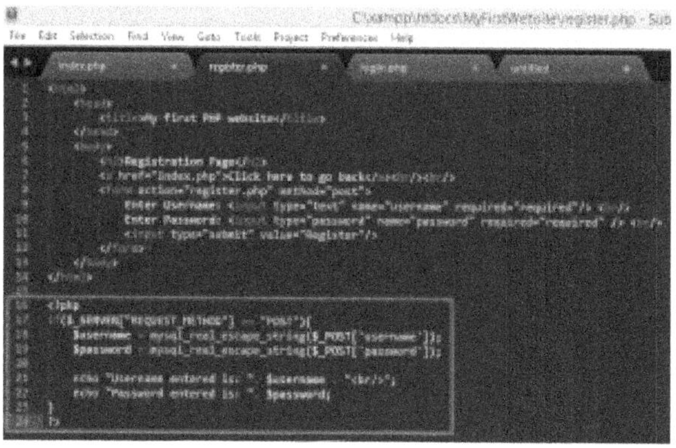

Here’s the amplification to the code:

```
<html>
<head>
<title>My first PHP Website</title>
</head>
<body>
<h2>Registration Page</h2>
<a href=”index.php”>Click here to go back<br/><br/>
<form action=”checklogin.php” method=”POST”>
        Enter Username: <input type=”text” name=”username” required=”required” /><br/>
        Enter password: <input type=”password” name=”password” required=”required” /><br/>
<input type=”submit” value=”Register”/>
</form>
</body>
</html>
```

$_SERVER[“REQUEST_METHOD”] == “POST” - checks if the structure has gotten a POST method when the submit button has been clicked. The POST method is made in html from the method=”POST.

$_POST['"] - gets the name originating from a POST method. This action basically gets the info with regards to the name from the structure. For our situation it's username and password.

mysql_real_escape_string() - exemplifies the information into a string to keep inputs from SQL Injections. This guarantees that your strings don't escape from extra characters.

After that, go to your register.php and attempt to input any data then click on "Register". For my situation I put in the username xtian and password as 123456. It ought to show the inputs below. Here's my specimen:

Through this part you ought to have seen on the most proficient method to get info through the structure and how to add it to the database. On your register.php, include the supplementary code:

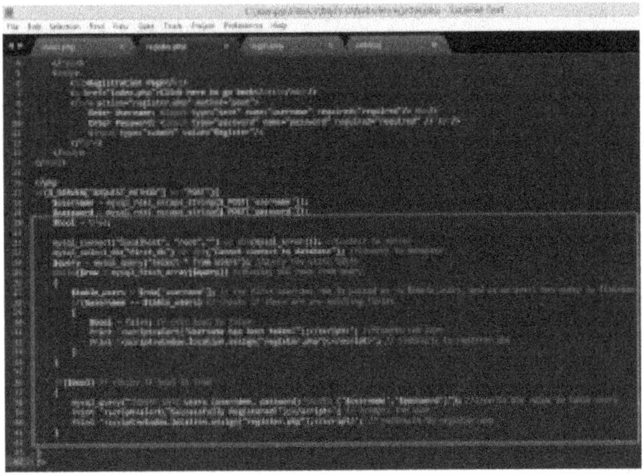

Here are the clarifications to the code:

```
<html>

<head>

<title>My first PHP Website</title>

</head>

<body>

<h2>Registration Page</h2>

<a href=”index.php”>Click here to go back<br/><br/>

<form action=”checklogin.php” method=”POST”>

        Enter Username: <input type=”text”
name=”username” required=”required” /><br/>

        Enter password: <input type=”password”
name=”password” required=”required” /><br/>
```

```
<input type="submit" value="Register"/>
</form>
</body>
</html>

alert("Username has been taken!");</script>'; //
Prompts the user
        Print '<script>window.location.
assign("register.php");</script>'; // redirects to regis-
ter.php
      }
   }

if($bool)
   {
mysql_query("INSERT INTO users (username,
password) VALUES ('$username', 'password')"); //
inserts value into table users
      Print '<script>alert("Successfully Regis-
tered!");</script>'; // Prompts the user
      Print '<script>window.location.assign("register.
php");</script>'; // redirects to register.php
   }
```

```
}
?>
```

mysql_connect("Server name","Server Username","Server Password") - The sentence structure used to join with our XAMPP server. localhost or 127.0.0.1 is the name of the server. The default username is root and no secret word for default.

mysql_select_db("database name") - Selects the database to be utilized.

then again die('Message') - Displays the lapse message if the condition wasn't met.

mysql_query('sql question') - does the SQL inquiries.

mysql_fetch_array('query') - brings all questions in the table to show or control data. It is put in a as a circle so that it would question all columns. Observe that, just 1 line is questioned per circle that is the reason a while circle is vital.

$row['row name'] - the estimation of the section in the present inquiry. It is represented as an exhibit. For our situation $row is the name of the variable for our column on the up and down.

Attempt the inputs that you have made before and see what happens. It ought to show that you have effectively registered. Attempt going to phpmyadmin and see your clients table:

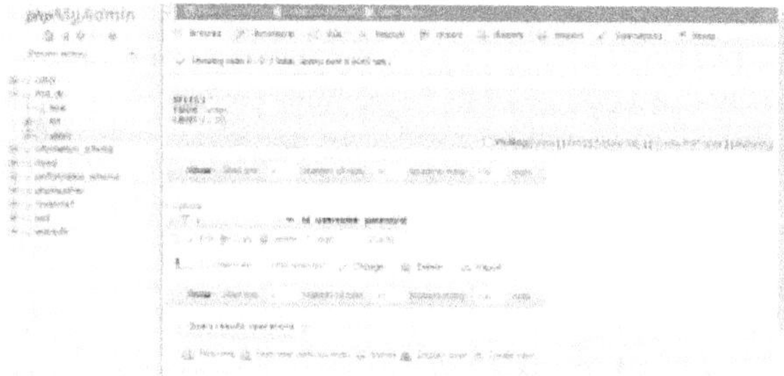

Congrats! Now you know how to include data into the database with data validations.

1.4 **User log-in: Authentication**

Subsequently, for the login page, we should make another document called checklogin.php. The reason is backtracking to our login.php, our structure has an activity called "checklogin.php", especially <form activity = "checklogin.php" method= "POST">. In the event that you will see it on the register.php, it's also on register.php because the back-end is done on the same document too.

How about we now code the checklogin.php with the accompanying language:

checklogin.php

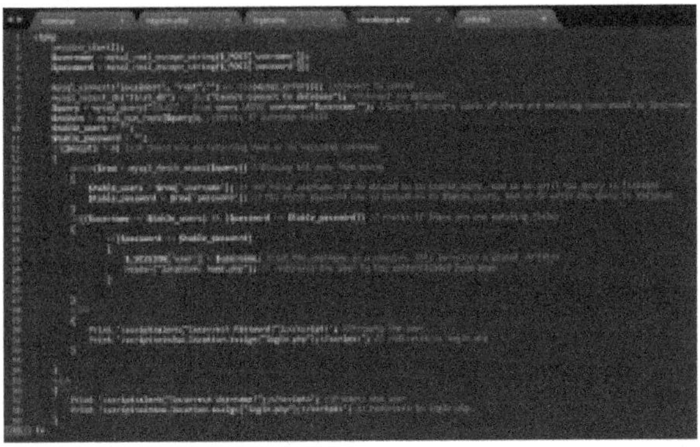

```
<?php
session_start();
    $username = mysql_real_escape_string($_POST[‘username’]);
    $password = mysql_real_escape_string($_POST[‘password’]);
    $bool = true;

mysql_connect(“localhost”, “root”, “”) or die (mysql_error()); //Connect to server
mysql_select_db(“first_db”) or die (“Cannot connect to database”); //Connect to database
    $query = mysql_query(“Select * from users WHERE username=’$username’”); // Query the users table
```

```
$exists = mysql_num_rows($query); //Checks if username exists

$table_users = "":

$table_password = "";

if($exists > 0) //IF there are no returning rows or no existing username

{

while($row = mysql_fetch_assoc($query)) // display all rows from query

    {

        $table_users = $row['username']; // the first username row is passed on to $table_users, and so on until the query is finished

        $table_password = $row['password']; // the first password row is passed on to $table_password, and so on until the query is finished

    }

if(($username == $table_users) && ($password == $table_password))// checks if there are any matching fields

    {

if($password == $table_password)

        {
```

```
$_SESSION['user'] = $username; //set the
username in a session. This serves as a global variable

header("location: home.php"); // redirects the user to
the authenticated home page

    }

  }

else

  {

    Print '<script>alert("Incorrect Password!");</
script>'; // Prompts the user

    Print '<script>window.location.assign("login.
php");</script>'; // redirects to login.php

  }

 }

else

 {

    Print '<script>alert("Incorrect username!");</
script>'; // Prompts the user

    Print '<script>window.location.assign("login.
php");</script>'; // redirects to login.php

 }

?>
```

session_start() - Starts the session. This is normally done on established pages. The reason why we used this is because it is needed for the $_SESSION[‘’].

mysql_num_rows() - This yields a whole number. This numbers every one of the columns depending on the inquiry.

$_SESSION[‘name’] - Serves as the session name for the whole session. This is more or less like open variables in item arranged programming. We will be utilizing this for recognizing whether the client is validated or not.

Then attempt to test your data with a wrong username and password. It ought to give back the preferred prompt. After testing, try inputting the right values. It ought to lead you to home.php.

Note: home.php does not exist yet so it will create an error 404.

CHAPTER 2

SETTING UP THE HOME PAGE FOR LOGGED-IN USERS AND LOGGING-OUT

Now that were confirmed, let now make our landing page (home.php) with the accompanying syntax:

home.php

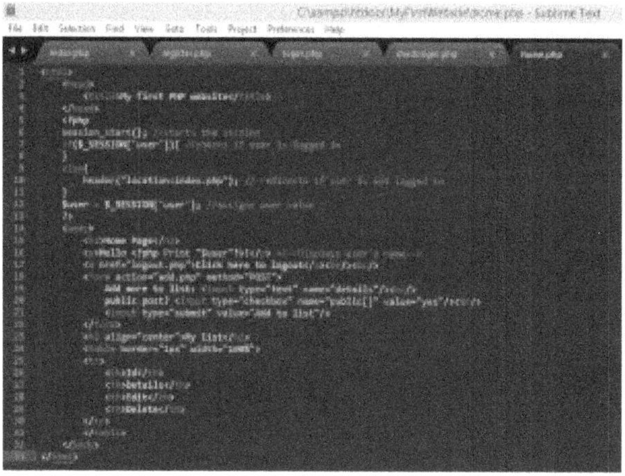

CODE ABOVE:

```
<html>

<head>

<title>My first PHP Website</title>
```

```
</head>
<?php
session_start(); //starts the session
if($_SESSION['user']){ // checks if the user is logged
in
  }
else{
header("location: index.php"); // redirects if user is
not logged in
  }
  $user = $_SESSION['user']; //assigns user value
  ?>
<body>
<h2>Home Page</h2>

<hello>!
<!--Display's user name-->
<a href="logout.php">Click here to go logout</
a><br/><br/>
<form action="add.php" method="POST">
        Add more to list: <input type="text"
name="details" /><br/>
```

```
        Public post? <input type=”checkbox”
name=”public[]” value=”yes” /><br/>
<input type=”submit” value=”Add to list”/>
</form>
<h2 align=”center”>My list</h2>

</body></html>
```

Here’s the explanation to the code:

session_start() - Basically starts the session. Required for $_SESSION[‘’].

header() - redirects the user.

Try refreshing your browser and it should look like this:

Now that we have our homepage, let’s try creating our logout.php and test if the user’s session is off. What we will ensure is that if the user is logged-out, the user shouldn’t access home.php. So here’s the simple syntax to logout.php:

logout.php

2.1 Testing Page Security

To test page security, try refreshing home.php and click on logout. Now try clicking on the back arrow of your program and see what happens:

As it should be clear, it doesn't guide you to home.php because you are logged-out. Then for the second test, attempt physically inputting the location localhost/MyFirstWebsite/home.php. The same case ought to happen as well. Since were logged-out, even a manual info of the location doesn't get to an approved page. What we have done is a simple security component in which we divert unapproved clients to an open page.

Now try signing in again and you should go back to home.php.

2.2 Adding data to the list - User Access Only

In our next step, how about we make the adding of data to the list to be user access only? As you will see from the structure, it is composed as <form action=”add.php” method=”POST”>, denoting that our http post request goes to add.php and with that, we make our add.php with the accompanying syntax:

CODE ABOVE:

```
<?php
session_start();
if($_SESSION['user']){
   }
else{
header("location:index.php");
   }

   $details = mysql_real_escape_string($_
POST['details']);
   $time = strftime("%X"); //time
   $date = strftime("%B %d, %Y"); //date
```

```
    Print "$time - $date - $details";
?>
```

Note that this isn't our certified add.php syntax yet, I'm simply going to show the time and date syntax and getting your data.

After that, do a reversal to your home.php and attempt to include an item then select "Add to list".

As should be obvious from the image, we have our current time, date, and your data. Here's the clarification to the code:

strftime() - get's the time in light of what arrangement your set.

> %X - current framework time.
>
> %B - current framework month.
>
> %d - current framework day.
>
> %Y - current framework year.

Now we should change our add.php and include the accompanying data into the database together with the data from the checkbox:

Here's a little clarification:

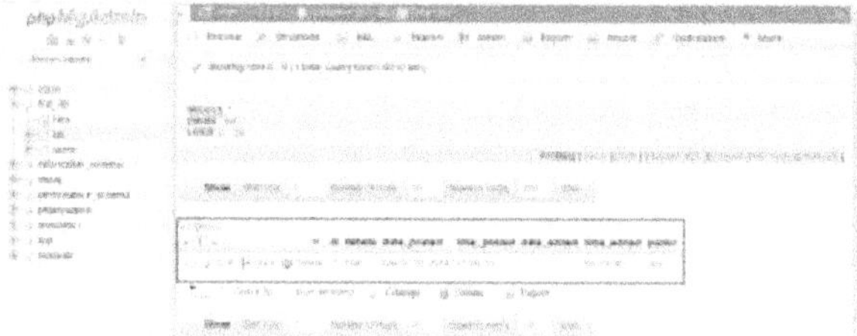

foreach() - gets the value of the checkbox. As you will see, the checkbox design in the structure is name="checkbox[]". To get data from checkbox, it must be instantiated as an array. Doing as such would make it feasible to get data from different checkboxes.

Now try at entering some data and click "Add to list". For my situation, I'll simply utilize fish once more. How about we go to our phpmyadmin and how about we check whether the data has been included? The results of my case are in the chapter below.

CHAPTER 3

DISPLAYING DATA IN THE HOME PAGE

Since we have seen that the information has been effectively included, we should now show the information in our landing page. We should change our home.php and how about we include a few sections for the date?

home.php

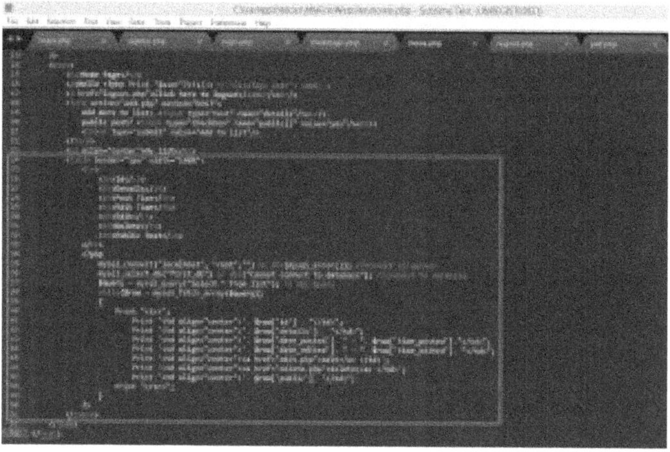

```
<html>

<head>
```

```
<title>My first PHP Website</title>
</head>
<?php
session_start(); //starts the session
if($_SESSION[‘user’]){ // checks if the user is logged in
  }
else{
header(“location: index.php”); // redirects if user is not logged in
  }
  $user = $_SESSION[‘user’]; //assigns user value
  ?>
<body>
<h2>Home Page</h2>

<hello>!
<!--Display’s user name-->
<a href=”logout.php”>Click here to go logout</a><br/><br/>
<form action=”add.php” method=”POST”>
```

```
        Add more to list: <input type=”text”
name=”details” /><br/>
        Public post? <input type=”checkbox”
name=”public[]” value=”yes” /><br/>
<input type=”submit” value=”Add to list”/>
</form>
<h2 align=”center”>My list</h2>
   ‘;
          Print ‘”;
          Print ‘”;
          Print ‘”;
          Print ‘”;
          Print ‘’;
          Print ‘’;
          Print ‘’;
       Print ‘’;
   }
  ?>
```

It should now show that information. From our CRUD agenda, we have now achieved Create and Read. Next is to update (edit) and erase data in case you find that we have alter and erase connections showed on the segment. I'll add another information to the list named "fish" to have another sample and this time, its privacy status is no:

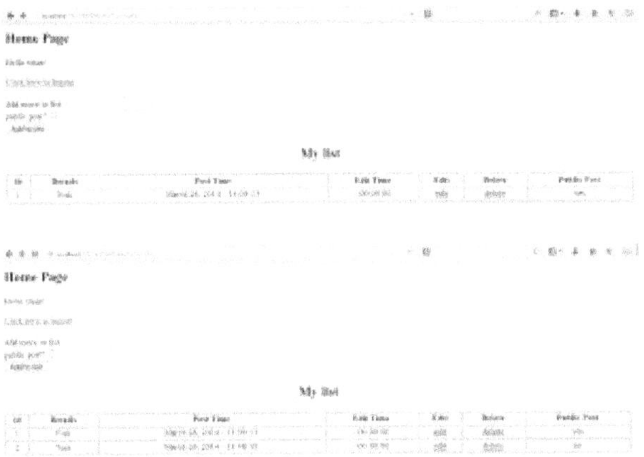

3.1 Editing Data

We should now try altering our information and to do that we will need to utilize another function called "GET". With our past routines, we have been utilizing POST as our http request but this time we will utilize GET for altering and erasing records. To begin with, we should change our home.php and add a little code to 2 segments:

home.php

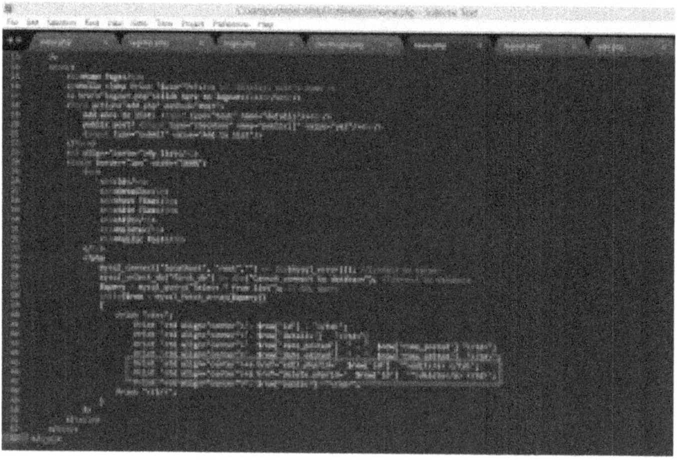

CODE ABOVE:

```
<html>
<head>
<title>My first PHP Website</title>
</head>
<?php
session_start(); //starts the session
if($_SESSION['user']){ // checks if the user is logged in
  }
else{
```

```
header("location: index.php"); // redirects if user is not logged in
  }
  $user = $_SESSION['user']; //assigns user value
  ?>
<body>
<h2>Home Page</h2>

<hello>!
<!--Display's user name-->
<a href="logout.php">Click here to go logout</a><br/><br/>
<form action="add.php" method="POST">
        Add more to list: <input type="text" name="details" /><br/>
        Public post? <input type="checkbox" name="public[]" value="yes" /><br/>
<input type="submit" value="Add to list"/>
</form>
<h2 align="center">My list</h2>
   ';
        Print '';
```

```
        Print '";
        Print '";
        Print '";
        Print '';
        Print '';
        Print '';
      Print '';
    }
  ?>
```

As you have seen, we just included URL parameter for the alter and erase interfaces to be for a specific ID. We will be utilizing this later to handle the information. The motivation behind why we use ID is on the grounds that it's an exceptional identifier. It is possible for the individual to have entered the same information so it's not advisable to utilize the *details* as a method of control later on.

Try putting your cursor into the edit link and you will see the estimation of the ID on the lower left:

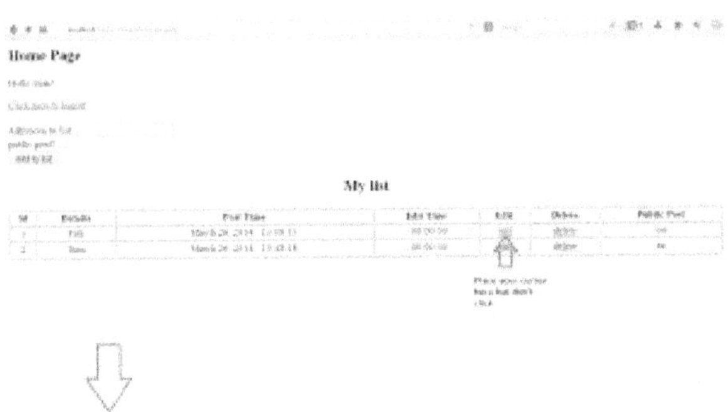

 Enter new detail: <input type="text" name="details"/>
 open post? <input type="checkbox name="public[]" value="yes"/><input type="submit" value="Update List"/></form> '; } else { <h2 align="center">There is not information to be edited.</h2> } ?></body></html> Click here for the complete edit.php code (Only allude to the front-end code.

```
<html>

<head>

<title>My first PHP Website</title>

</head>

<?php

session_start(); //starts the session

if($_SESSION['user']){ // checks if the user is logged in
```

```
  }
else{
header("location: index.php"); // redirects if user is not logged in
  }
  $user = $_SESSION['user']; //assigns user value
  ?>
<body>
<h2>Home Page</h2>

<hello>!
<!--Display's user name-->
<a href="logout.php">Click here to go logout</a><br/><br/>
<a href="home.php">Return to home page</a>
<h2 align="center">Currently Selected</h2>
   0)
       {
while($row = mysql_fetch_array($query))
         {
```

Some explanations to the code:

!empty() - a method that checks if the value is not empty. The syntax can be reversed if you want to check if it's empty by removing the explanation point (!), therefore it's syntax would be empty().

$_GET[''] - Used to get the value from the parameter. In our case, we use id as our URL parameter so the syntax would be $_GET['id'].

$id_exists - the variable that checks whether the given id exists.

$_SESSION['id'] - we place the value of id into session to use it on another file.

Lines 42-76

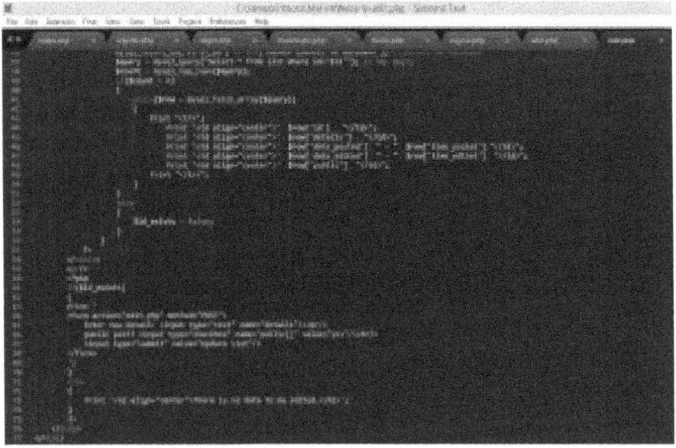

How about we attempt adjusting the URL parameter by getting rid of ?id=1. This should result to localhost/MyFirstWebsite/edit.php and it ought to result like this:

edit.php?id=1

Go ahead and click Update list and you should be redirected to *home.php* and see the updated list.

Since we secured our URL parameters, lets now put the alter syntax. We should backpedal to edit.php and add some complementary code to restore the data to the database:

Congrats! We have now done the edit function!

3.2 Deleting data

Taking a look back to the CRUD, we have now done creating (adding), reading (displaying), and updating (editing) records. At this point, the last part is erasing records. For this part, it’s generally the same as what we have done on edit, however, what varies is only the SQL statement. Rather than utilizing UPDATE, we will be utilizing the DELETE syntax. In erasing records, we need to prompt individuals verifying that they’d truly need to erase the record so we will be including a little JavaScript in home.php. To do that, we should alter our code and include some int. home.php

home.php

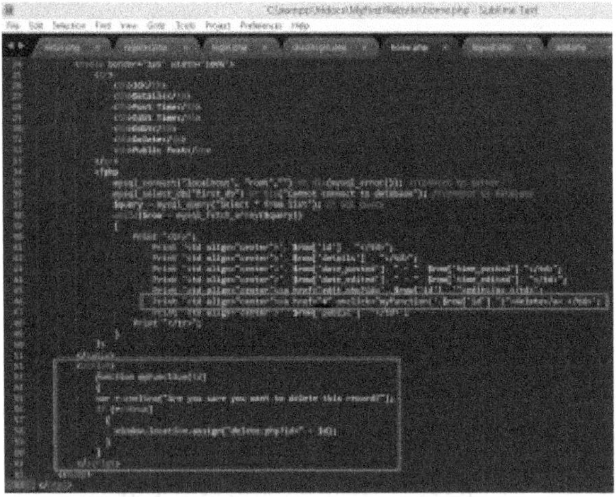

CODE ABOVE:

```
<table border="1px" width="100%">

    Id
    Details
    Post Time
    Edit Time
    Edit
    Delete
    Public Post

  ';
        Print ''. $row['id'] . "";
        Print ''. $row['details'] . "";
        Print ''. $row['date_posted'] . " - " .
$row['time_posted'] . "";
        Print ''. $row['date_edited'] . " - " .
$row['time_edited'] ."";
        Print '<a href="edit.
php?id='.$row['id'].'">edit';
        Print '<a href="#" nclick="myfunction('.$ro
w['id'].')">delete</a>';
```

```
            Print ''. $row['public'] . '';
        Print '';
    }
  ?>




<script>
function myFunction(id)
  {
var r = confirm("Are you sure you want to delete this record?");
if(r == true)
    {
window.location.assign("delete.php?id=" + id);
    }
  }
</script>
```

As you have seen, we altered the link for the delete. We changed href into "#" and included and onclick capacity for JavaScript for the technique for myFunction and inside it's parameter is the id of the row. Below the table composed is the JavaScript syntax wherein it prompts the user on the off chance that he/she need's to erase the record. In case the client affirms, the page then connects to delete.php together embedded with the value of the id. Next, let us make delete.php and here's the accompanying syntax:

Delete.php

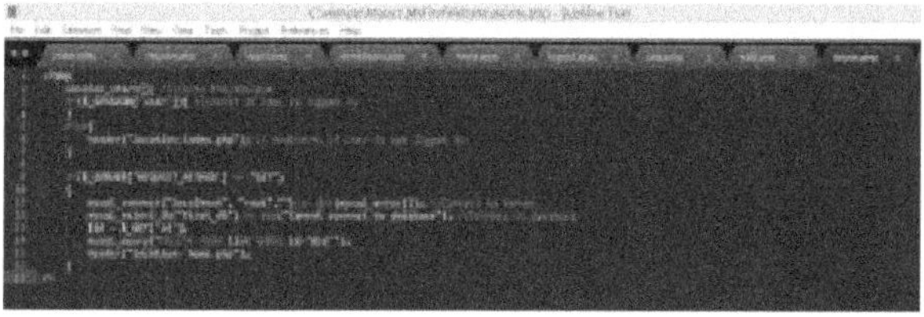

CODE ABOVE:

```
<?php
session_start(); //starts the session
if($_SESSION['user']){ //checks if user is logged in
   }
else {
header("location:index.php"); //redirects if user is not logged in.
   }
```

```
if($_SERVER['REQUEST_METHOD'] == "GET")
   {
mysql_connect("localhost", "root", "") or die(mysql_
error()); //connect to server
mysql_select_db("first_db") or die("cannot connect to
database"); //Connect to database
      $id = $_GET['id'];
mysql_query("DELETE FROM list WHERE
id='$id'");
header("location:home.php");
   }
?>
```

The code is simply straightforward and the syntax is as well the ones that we utilized before although you may notice we have changed our request technique into GET. At this stage, we are utilizing the GET request since we have a URL parameter. Now try refreshing home.php and let us attempt erasing the first record. This ought to be the outcome:

Prompting:

End-result:

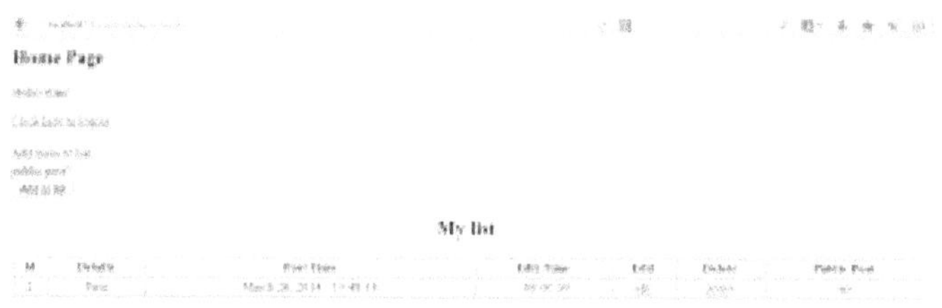

Congrats! At this point we have authoritatively finished our CRUD proclamations!

3.3 Displaying public data

Subsequently, let us see how public information should be play. We will be showing information that has been set to yes in our index.php, in which is a page for non-authenticated users. It's exceptionally simple. We simply need to alter our index.php and include some php code and table. Here's our upgraded index.php:

index.php

Now log-out and see your default page. It should look something like this:

Note: You won't see the data yet since we haven't set any information to public.

Now let's log-in again and this time, let's add some more data. In my case I've added the following:

Salad - public

Corn - non-public

Pasta - public

Chicken - public

Spaghetti - non-public

With a total of 6 data's with 3 of each privacy setting:

home.php

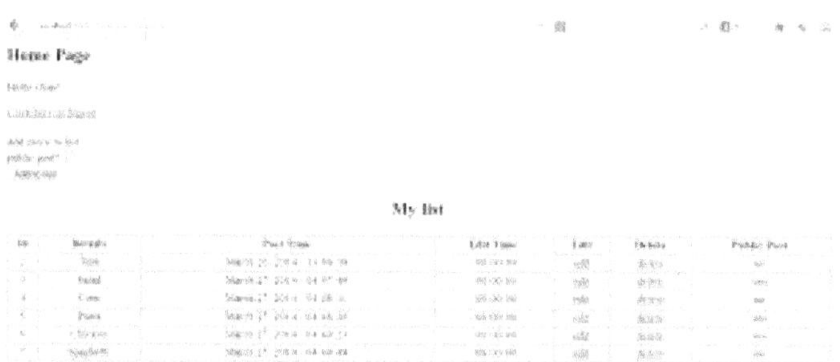

Now let's log-out and see our default page (index.php). It should now look like this:

index.php

As you can see, it only displays data that are set to public.

CHAPTER 4

DYNAMIC CONTENT AND THE WEB

To the normal client, a web page is simply just a web page. It opens in the browser and gives information. Looking closer, however, various pages stay for the most part the same, while other pages change routinely. Pages that don't change—static pages—are generally simple to make. Somebody needs to make a HTML archive doc, by hand or with apparatuses/tools, and transfer it to a website where web browsers can visit. A standout amongst the most well-known instruments to make HTML docs is Adobe Dreamweaver. At the point when changes are required, you simply supplant the old file with another one. Dynamic pages are made with HTML as well, although, rather than a basic build and-post approach, the pages are upgraded routinely, even sometimes every time that they are asked.

Static sites give hyperlinked text and maybe a login screen, however, past that they don't offer much association. By contrast, Amazon.com (http://www.amazon.com) exhibits a lot of what a dynamic site can do: your ordering information is logged plus Amazon offers suggestions taking into account your buying history when you access their page. At the end of the day, dynamic implies that the client interacts with the site past simply perusing pages, and the site responds in view of your activities. Going through each page is a personalized experience.

Making dynamic pages—even a couple of years ago—implied composition of a considerable amount of code in the C or Perl dialects, and afterward calling and executing those programs through a procedure called a Common Gateway Interface (CGI). Nonetheless, making such executable files wasn't much fun, nor was taking in an entire new complex language.

Thankfully, PHP and MySQL ensure that making dynamic web sites is simpler and faster.

4.1 HTTP and the Internet

Some basic knowledge of how the Internet functions may be helpful on the off chance that you haven't programmed for the Web recently. The HyperText Transfer Protocol (HTTP) identifies how site pages are exchanged over the Internet. HTTP is the system used to exchange or pass on data on the World Wide Web. Its unique reason for existing was to give an approach to publish, distribute and recover HTML pages. The World Wide Web Consortium (W3C) and the Internet Engineering Task Force harmonized the development of HTTP, which are request-and-response protocols that join customers and servers. The client at the starting point, normally a web browser, is alluded to as the *user agent*. The destination server, which stores or builds resources as well as enclosing HTML documents and pictures, is known as the *original server*. Between the user agents and root server, there may be a few intermediaries such as proxies. A HTTP customer starts a request by setting up a Transmission Control Protocol (TCP) connection to a specific port on a remote host (port 80 is the default). An HTTP server listening on that port waits for the customer to send a request message.

After accepting the request, the server sends back a status line, as "HTTP/1.1 200 Alright," and its own particular response. Contingent upon the status, this reactional response could be the request file, a error message, or some other data. HTTP is made on top of TCP, which is itself layered on top of Internet Protocol (IP).

The two are often together termed as TCP/IP. Applications on organized hosts can utilize TCP to make associations with each other, and afterward exchange of information. The protocol ensures solid conveyance of information from sender to collector. TCP underpins a hefty portion of the Internet's most prominent application protocols and applications, comprising of the Web, email, and Secure Shell (SSH).

4.2 PHP and MySQL's Place in Web Development

PHP is a programming language designed to create web pages interactively on the PC serving them, which is known as a *web server*. Dissimilar from HTML, where the web program uses tags and markup to create a page, PHP code keeps running between the requested page and the web server, adding to and changing the fundamental HTML output.

PHP makes web advancement simple in light of the fact that all the code you need is contained inside the PHP framework. This implies that there's no particular reason for you to reevaluate the wheel every time you sit to develop to a PHP program; it is accompanied by built-in web functionality. While PHP is awesome for web application development, it doesn't store data by itself. For that, you require a database. The database of CHOICE for PHP engineers is MySQL, which acts like a filing clerk for PHP-prepared user data. MySQL robotizes the most widely recognized tasks involving storing and recovering specific client data taking into account your supplied criteria. MySQL is effortlessly accessed from PHP, and they function admirably together. An included advantage is that PHP and MySQL keep running on different PC types and working frameworks, including Mac OS X, Windows-based PCs, and Linux. Several elements make utilizing PHP and MySQL together the natural decision by many:

- *PHP and MySQL function well together*

PHP and MySQL have been created on account of one another in mind, so they are simple to utilize together. The programming interfaces between them are sensibly paired up. The idea of these two working together wasn't an idea in addendum when the designers made thenPHP and MySQL interfaces.

- *PHP and MySQL have open source power*

As they are both open source tasks, PHP and MySQL can both be utilized for free. MySQL customer libraries are no longer packaged with PHP. Advanced clients can make improvements to the source code, and along those lines change the way the language and computer programs work.

- *PHP and MySQL have group support*

Both of them have dynamic communities on the Web in which you can take an interest, and the members will help you answer your inquiries. You can likewise buy proficient support for MySQL in the event that you require it.

- *PHP and MySQL are fast*

Their basic and efficient designs empower speedier processing.

- *PHP and MySQL don't impede you with superfluous details*

The Value of Open Source

As we said above, both PHP and MySQL are both open source projects, so you need not to worry about purchasing user licenses for each PC in your office or home. At any point when using open source projects and technologies, most programmers usually have access to the source code. This facilitates individual or even group analysis to distinguish probable complex code, debug, test, and offer changes and additions to that code.

For instance, Unix - the precursor in the open source programming community—was openly shared with college programming researchers. Linux, the free alternative for Unix, is an immediate outcome of their endeavors and the open source-licensing model. Generally, open source licenses consist of the privilege to distribute adjusted code but with a few limitations. For instance, a few licenses necessitate that derivative code should be release under the same license, or there may be a limitation that others can't utilize your code.

Open source licensing started as an endeavor to safeguard a culture of sharing, and later prompted an extended awareness regarding the value of that sharing. Today, open source software engineers share their code changes on the Web by means of http://www.php.net, listservs, and websites. In case you find yourself in a coding nightmare which you can't awaken, the resources mentioned in this chapter can and will help.

4.3 The Components of a PHP Application

If your end goal to transform and create dynamic web pages, you'll have to comprehend and use a few technologies. There are three principle parts of making dynamic web pages: a web server, a server-side programming language, and a database. It's a smart idea to have an in-depth understanding of these three essential parts for web development when using PHP. We'll begin with some simple comprehension of the history also, motivation behind Apache (your web server), PHP (your server-side programming dialect), also, MySQL (your database). This can help you to see how they fit into the web advancement picture. Keep in mind that dynamic web pages pull data from a few sources at the same time, including Apache, PHP, MySQL, and Cascading Style Sheets (CSS), which we'll discuss later.

PHP

PHP developed out of a need for individuals to create and keep up web sites containing dynamic customer-server functionality. In 1998, PHP was discharged in its third form, transforming it into a web advancement apparatus that could compete with similar items like, Microsoft's Active Server Pages (ASP) and Sun's Java Server Pages (JSP). PHP additionally is an interpreted language, instead of an assembled one. The genuine magnificence of PHP is its straightforwardness combined with its power.

PHP is almost everywhere and is very compatible with all major operating systems. It is also simple to learn, making it a perfect tool for web programming beginners. Furthermore, you get to exploit a group's push to make web development simpler for everybody.

The makers of PHP added to a foundation that permits experienced C developers to expand PHP's capacities. Consequently, PHP now incorporates cutting edge innovations like XML, XSL, and Microsoft's Component Object Model Technologies (COM).

Apache

Apache is a web server that transforms program requests into consequential web pages and knows how to process PHP code. PHP is just a programming language, so without the force of a web server like Apache behind it, there would be no chance to getting web clients to reach your pages containing the PHP code. Apache is not by any means the only web server accessible. Another well known web server is Microsoft's Internet Information Services (IIS), which is supplied with Windows 2000 and every later form. Apache has several distinct advantages of being free, giving full source code, and utilizing an unrestricted license. Apache 2.0 is the present version you would doubtlessly be using, however, 1.3 is still frequently being utilized. IIS is simpler to coordinate with Active Directory, Microsoft's most recent authentication framework; however, this applies generally to internal organization websites.

Since web servers like Apache and IIS are designed to serve up HTML records, they need a user to know how to prepare PHP code. Apache utilizes modules to load expansions into its functionality. IIS utilizes an analogous concept called Internet Server Application Program Interface (ISAPI). These both take into consideration quicker preparation of the PHP code than the old-school procedure of calling PHP as a different executable every time the web server had a request for a page containing PHP. We'll talk about how the Apache module setup in the next chapter.

Apache has just two noteworthy versions being used today: 1.3 and 2. Apache 2 is a big rework of 1.3 which supports *threading*. Threads enable just one process to oversee more than one thing at a particular instance. This builds speed and lessens the resources required. Sadly, PHP isn't absolutely compatible with threading yet. Apache 2 has been out long enough to be viewed as secure for use in development and creation situations.

Apache 2 supports more effective modules as well. Nonetheless, shared module DLLs that don't accompany the official Apache source records, for example, *mod_php4, mod_ ssl, mod_auth_mysql, and mod_ auth_ntsec*, can be found on the Web. Apache similarly has the upside of having the capacity to keep running on other operating systems other than Windows, which now takes us to the subject of compatibility. However, first we'll give you a little more exhaustive coverage of relational databases and SQL.

SQL and Relational Databases

Organized Query Language (SQL) is the most famous language used to make, recover, overhaul, and erase information from relational database administration frameworks. A *relational* database complies with the relational model and alludes to a database's information as well as schema. The *schema* is the database's structure of how information is organized. Regular use of the expression "Relational Database Management System" actually alludes to the programming used to make a relational database, for example, Oracle or Microsoft SQL Server. A relational database is a compilation of tables, yet different items are regularly considered some part of the database, as they help sort out and structure the information as well as forcing the database to fit in with an the set of predetermined requirements.

MySQL

MySQL is a free relational database which still contains full-features. MySQL was created in the 1990s to fill the continually developing requirement for PCs to oversee data shrewdly. The first core MySQL designers were attempting to unravel their need for a database by utilizing mSQL, a very small and basic database. It turned out to be clear that mSQL couldn't take care of the considerable number of issues they needed it to, so they made a more robust database that transformed into MySQL.

MySQL bolsters a few distinctive *database engines*. Database engines decide how MySQL handles the real stockpiling and querying of the information. Due to that, each storage engine has its own particular arrangement of capabilities and strengths. After some time, the database engines accessible are turning out to be more progressive and quicker.

The latest production release of MySQL is the 5.0x version. MySQL 5.0 gives execution that is similar to any of the a great deal more costly undertaking databases for example, Oracle, Informix, DB2 (IBM), and SQL Server (Microsoft). The developers have accomplished this level of performance execution by utilizing the talents of numerous open source designers, alongside community testing. For general web-driven database tasks, the default MyISAM database engine works exceptionally fine. Don't worry over the most recent and most prominent elements of databases, as the greater part of what you'll likely need has already been incorporated in MySQL for quite a while.

Compatibility

Web programs, for example, Safari, Firefox, Netscape, and Internet Explorer are made to process HTML, so it doesn't make a difference which operating systems a web server keeps running on. Apache, PHP, and

MySQL bolster an extensive variety of operating systems (OS), so you aren't limited to a particular OS on either the server or the customer. While you don't need to stress much over software compatibility, the sheer assortment of file formats as well as diverse languages that all meet up does take some getting used to.

4.4 Integrating Many Sources of Information

In the beginning of the Web, life was easy. Files contained HTML as well as binary files, for example, pictures. A few advances have subsequently been created to improve the look of web pages. For instance, Cascading Style Sheets (CSS) pull presentation data out of your HTML and into a solitary spot with the goal that you can make formatting changes over a whole arrangement of pages at the same time; you don't need to physically change your HTML markup one HTML page at once.

You can possibly have data from HTML documents that reference CSS, PHP templates, and a MySQL database at the same time. PHP templates make it simpler to change the HTML in a page when it contains fields populated by a database query.

Just to get an essence of what your code will resemble, it will be good to look at an example which contains PHP code that creates HTML from a MySQL database, and that HTML itself alludes to a CSS style sheet.

The outcome is that while you've added another document to the blend, you've made the HTML markup simpler to read, and the PHP code is less jumbled with incidental HTML. A web designer who's not gifted in PHP can adjust the look of the page without stressing over breaking the PHP code.

The last kind of data indicated here, CSS, additionally originates from an aspiration to isolate the presentation styles, for example, content and colors from the important content.

Cascading Style Sheets (CSS) supplements HTML to give web designers and clients more control over the way their web pages show. Designers and clients can make style sheets that characterize how diverse components, for example, headers and links, show up on the web website. The term cascading infers from the actuality that numerous style sheets at distinctive levels can be connected to the same web page with definitions acquiring from one level to the next. To apply CSS code, the illustration code indicated is put inside the header of your HTML record.

```
<html>

<head>

<title>CSS Example</title>

<style type="text/css">

h4, b {color: #80D92F; text style family: arial; }
```

```
p { content indent: 2cm; foundation: yellow; text style family: courier;}

</style>

</head>

<body>

<h3>Learn how to utilize CSS on your web sites!</h3>

<h4>It’s cool, it’s stunning, it even spares you time!</h4>

<p>Isn’t this <b>nifty</b>?</p>

</body>

</html>
```

In the CSS, you can either designate a color by naming it, as we did here with the backdrop designation, “background: yellow”, or you can appoint it with a numeric color code, as we did here, “color #80D92F”. The code that starts with style is the CSS code.

In spite of the fact that we incorporate the CSS in the record in this sample, it could originate from a different document, where it can be referenced as user_admin.css.

All things considered, it’s a matter of style. We make use of upper case in our web destinations so we can see the HTML better and put a carriage return between every markup line. Labels commonly happen in start-end sets.

These pairs are in the following structure: *<tag>Isn't this nifty?</tag>*

The initial <tag> shows the start of a label pair, and the last </tag> demonstrates the end. This complete pair of labels is called an *element*. Any substance inside of an element has the principles of the element connected to it. In the earlier sample, the text "Learn how to utilize CSS on your web sites!" is contained by a h3 component: *<h3>Learn how to utilize CSS on your web sites!</h3>*

It's additionally great practice (and it's needed by XHTML) that your labels settle neatly to produce elements with clear limits. Continuously utilize end tags when you achieve the end of an element, and abstain from having sets of tags that cover. (Rather than <b>bold<i> italic</i></b>, you ought to close the code like this: </b></i>.) At the end of the day, you should open and close things at the same level. Along these lines, on the off chance that you open a bold and after that italic, you ought to close the italic before you close the bold.

4.5 Requesting Data from a Web Page

It can be precarious to see how these pieces incorporate each other. At the point when a web server identifies PHP code, it turns over the handling of the page to the PHP interpreter. The server processes the PHP record and sends the subsequent HTML document to the server. On the off chance that the result incorporates an external CSS style sheet, the program issues a different request for that style sheet before putting the page on display.

Handling PHP on the server is called *server-side processing*. When you ask for a web page, you trigger an entire chain of reactions. Figure represents this association between your PC and the web server, which is the host of the web website.

Here is the process of server-side processing:

1. You enter a web page address in your browser's location bar.

2. Your browser separates that address and sends the name of the page to the web server. For instance, *http://www.phone.com/directory.html* would request the page directory.html from www.phone.com.

3. A program on the web server, called the web server process, takes the request for *directory.htm*l and searches for this particular file.

4. The web server reads the *directory.html* from the web server's hard drive.

5. The web server gives back the content of directory.html to your browser.

6. Your web program utilizes the HTML markup that was returned from the web server to construct the interpretation of the web page on your PC screen.

The HTML file named directory.html is known as a *static web page* on the grounds that everybody who requests the *directory.html* page gets precisely the same page.

For the web server to alter the returned page, PHP and MySQL are added to the blend.

Every step in that process is recorded here:

1. You enter a web page address in your browser's location bar.

2. Your program separates that address and sends the name of the page to the host. Case in point, http://www.phone.com/login.php requests the page login.php from www.phone.com.

3. The web server process on the host gets the solicitation for login.php.

4. The web server reads the login.php record from the host's hard drive.

5. The web server recognizes that the PHP file isn't only a plain HTML document, so it inquires another procedure—the PHP interpreter—processes the document.

6. The PHP interpreter executes the PHP code that it finds in the content it got from the web server process.

Included in that code are calls to the MySQL database.

7. PHP asks the MySQL database process to execute the database calls.

8. The MySQL database process sends back the results of the database query.

9. The PHP translator finishes execution of the PHP code with the information from the database and returns the outcomes to the web server process.

10. The web server gives back the outcomes as HTML content to your browser.

11. Your web browser utilizes the returned HTML content to assemble the web page on your screen.

This may appear like a considerable measure of steps, yet the majority of this processing happens naturally each time a web page with PHP code is requested. Indeed, this procedure may happen a few times for a single web page, since a web page can contain numerous image files as well as the CSS definition, which should all be recovered from the web server.

Whilst creating dynamic web pages, you work with an assortment of variables and server components, which are essential to having an alluring, maintainable, simple to-navigate, also, viable website.

In the next chapter, we demonstrate to you installation procedures and introduce a noteworthy cogs required to make this work i.e. PHP

CHAPTER 5

EXPLORING PHP

With PHP, MySQL, and Apache introduced, you're prepared to start writing code. Dissimilar to numerous languages, PHP doesn't need complex devices such as compilers and debuggers. Actually, you'll soon see that you can enter PHP directly into your current HTML docs, and with only a couple of changes, you'll be off and running.

In this chapter, we'll begin by demonstrating to you how PHP handles basic text, and afterward proceed to essential decision-making. Some truly cool things you can do include drawing a picture based the current client's browser, and printing a warning message if the client is working from an operating system that makes your website look crummy. This and more is conceivable with PHP, which makes these traps easy to navigate.

5.1 PHP and HTML Text

It's easy to output content using PHP; actually, handling content is one of PHP's fortes. We'll start with detailing where PHP is processed, then take a look at a percentage of the essential functions to output text, and from there go directly into printing the text in view of a certain condition being valid.

Text Output

In your endeavor to learn PHP, you will need the ability to show message simply and regularly. PHP gives you a chance to do that, however you'll have to utilize legitimate PHP syntax when making the code. Or else, your browser will assume that everything is HTML and produces the PHP code specifically to the browser. Everything will look like a content and code mix up. This will surely bring confusion to clients of your website! You can utilize whichever text editor you like to compose your PHP code, including Notepad or DevPHP (http://sourceforge.net/ventures/devphp/).

Our instances show how comparative HTML markup and PHP code look, and what you can do to begin noticing the contrasts between them.

5.1 PHP and HTML Text

In spite of the fact that most code looks really basic, it really wouldn't fill in as it is, so there are a few problems. There's no real way to tell in a file which part is standard HTML as well as which part is PHP. Consequently, the echo ( ) order must be handled of in a different manner. The fix is to encompass your PHP code with <?php ?> labels.

When you begin composing PHP code, you'll be working with easy text files that contain PHP and HTML code. HTML is a basic markup language that designates how your page looks in a browser; however, it is just that: text only. The server doesn't have to transform HTML documents before sending them to the client's browser. Contrasting HTML code, PHP code must be deciphered before the resulting page is sent to the browser. If not, the outcome will be one major mess on the client's screen.

To separate the PHP code to inform the web server what should be processed, the PHP code is put between formal or casual tags blended with HTML. The echo and print develops work very precisely the same, with the exception of echo can take more than one argument yet doesn't return any benefit, while *print* takes one argument. We picked *hello.php* as the filename; nonetheless, you can pick any name you like given that the length of the filename has the augmentation *.php*.

This tells the web server to process this document's PHP code.

5.2 Coding Building Blocks

To compose programs in PHP that do something helpful, you'll have to know blocks of reusable code called methods or function, and also how to temporarily store data that can't be executed in variables. We discuss *evaluations*, which permit your code to make astute choices in light of mathematical principles and user data.

Variables

Since we expect that some of you haven't done any programming, we get it that variables may be another idea. A *variable* stores a value, for example, the text string "Hi World!" or the integral value 1. A variable can then be reused all through your code, rather than needing to sort out the integral value again and again for the whole life of the variable, which can be disappointing and tiring.

Give careful consideration to some key elements that are in the form of variables. The dollar sign ($) should at all time fill the first space of your variable. The first character after the dollar sign must be either a letter or an underscore. It can't under any circumstances be a number; generally, your code won't execute, so watch those grammatical mistakes!

- PHP variables may be made just out of alphanumeric characters and underscores; for instance, a-z, A-Z, 0-9, and _.
- Variables in PHP are case-sensitive. This implies that $variable_name and $Variable_Name are different.
- Variables with more than a single word can be isolated with underscores to make them simpler to understand; for instance, $test_variable.
- Variables can be assigned values that use the equal

sign (=).

- Always end with a semicolon (;) to finish assigning the variable.

Reading a variable's value

To get to the value of a variable that has previously been assigned, just specify the dollar sign ($) followed by the variable name, and utilize it as you would the value of the variable in your code. You don't need to remove your variables when your program finishes. They're temporary since PHP naturally tidies them up when you finish using them.

- Variable types

Variables all store certain types of information. PHP naturally picks a data variable taking into account the value assigned. These information types comprise of strings, numbers, and also more complex components such as arrays. We'll talk about arrays later. What's vital to know is that unless you have motivation to care about the type of data. PHP handles all of the points of interest, so you don't have to stress over them. In circumstances where a particular sort of information is needed, for example, the numerical division operation, PHP endeavors to convert the data types naturally. In the event that you have a string with a single "2," it will be changed over to a whole number estimation of 2. This change is dependably exactly what you need PHP to do, and it makes coding consistent for you.

- Variable scope

PHP helps keep your code sorted out by verifying that on the off chance that you use code that somebody else composed (and you likely will), the names of the variables in your code don't clash with other beforehand composed variable names. For instance, in case you're utilizing a variable called $name that has an estimation of *Bill*, and you use another person's code that additionally has a variable called $name however utilizes it to stay informed concerning the filename log. txt, your worth could get overwritten. Your code's value for $name of Bill will be supplanted by log.txt, and your code will make say *Hello log.txt* rather than *Hello Bill*, which would be a major problem.

To keep this from happening, PHP sorts out code into functions. Functions permit you to gather a piece of code together and execute that code by its name. To keep variables in your code separate from variables in functions, PHP gives separate storage of variables inside of every function. This different storage room implies that the scope, or where a variable's value cab be admitted, is the nearby the local storage of the value.

- Global variables

Global variables permit you to cross the limit between discrete capacities to get to a variable's worth. The worldwide proclamation indicates that you need the variable to be the same variable everywhere that it is regarded as global.

Global variables ought to be utilized sparingly on the grounds that it's simple to unintentionally adjust a variable without acknowledging what the results are. This sort of error can be extremely hard to find. Also, when we examine functions in detail, you'll discover that you can send in values to functions when you call them and get values returned from them when they're done. You don't need to use global variables.

On the off chance that you need to use a variable in a particular function without losing the worth every time the function ends, however you would prefer not to use a global variable, but rather use a static variable.

- Static variables

Static variables give a variable that isn't decimated when a function ends. You can utilize the static variable value again whenever you call the capacity and it will have the same value as when it was last utilized as a part of the function. The easiest approach to consider this is to think about the variable as global yet open to simply that function. The estimation of $age is currently held every time the birthday function is called. The worth will stay around until the program ends. Value is spared on the grounds that it's announced as static. In this way, we've talked about two types of variables, yet there's still one more to examine, super globals.

- Super global variables

Super global variables, PHP uses uncommon variables called *super globals* to give data about the PHP script's surroundings. These variables don't require any announcement as global. They are habitually accessible, and they give imperative data past the script's code itself, for example, values from a user's input.

Since PHP 4.01, the super globals are termed as arrays. Arrays are unique accumulations of values that we'll talk about in later chapters. The more established super global variables such as those beginning with $HTTP_* that were not in clusters still exist, but rather their use is definitely not recommended, as they are deprecated.

CHAPTER 6

PHP DECISION-MAKING

In the last part you began learning programming with PHP and some code basics. Presently, it's chance to grow your comfort, learning, and knowledge of PHP. We'll begin with expressions and statatents.

6.1 Expressions

There are a few building blocks of coding that you have to comprehend: explanations, expressions, and operators. A *statement* is code that performs tasks. Statements are comprised of expressions and operators. An expression is a bit of code that assesses to a value. A worth can be a number, a string of content, or a Boolean.

An operator is a code component that follows up on an expression somehow. For example, a minus sign (–) can be used to tell the PC to decrement the value of the expression after it from the expression before it. Case in point:

$account_balance=$credits-$debits;

The most essential thing to see about expressions is the way to consolidate them into compound expressions and proclamations utilizing operators. In this way, we're going to look at operators used to transform expressions into more mind boggling expressions and statements.

The easiest type of expression is literal or a variable. An *literal* assesses to itself.

A few examples of literals are numbers, strings, and constants. A variable assesses to the worth allocated to it.

Despite the fact that a literal or variable may be a legitimate expression, they don't do anything. You get expressions to do things, for example, math or task by connecting them together with operators. An operator joins basic expressions into more intricate expressions by making connections between basic expressions that can be assessed. For example, if the connection you need to set up is the total joining of two numeric qualities together, you could compose 3 + 4. The numbers 3 and 4 are each substantial expressions. Including 3 + 4 is likewise a legitimate expression, whose value, for this situation, happens to be 7. The plus sign (+) is an operator. The numbers to either side of it are its arguments, or operands. Arguments or operand is something on which an operator takes action; for instance, an argument or operand could be a mandate from your housemate to discharge the dishwasher, and the administrator discharges the dishwasher. Distinctive operators have diverse types and numbers of operands. Administrators can likewise be over-burdened, which implies that they do distinctive things in distinctive contexts.

You've presumably speculated from this data that two or more expressions associated by operators are called an expression. You're right, as operators make complex expressions. The more sub-expressions and operators you have, the more drawn out and more mind boggling the expression. In any case, the length of it can be assigned to a value, it's still an expression.

At the point when expressions and operators are amassed to deliver a bit of code that really does something, you have a statement.

The operators are recorded as found on http://www.php.net/manual/en/language.operators. php. There are a few operators we're going to talk about so you can get up and running with PHP as fast as could possible. These incorporate a percentage of the throwing administrators that we'll just skim the surface of for the time being. Every operator has four basic properties in addition to its main functionality:

- Operator associativity
- Number of operands
- Order of precedence
- Types of operands

There truly isn't a great deal more to see about expressions with the exception of how to amass them into compound expressions and articulations using operators. Next, we're going to talk about operators that are utilized to transform expressions into more intricate expressions and statements.

6.2 Operator Concepts

PHP has numerous sorts of administrators/operators, including:

- Arithmetic administrators
- Array administrators
- Assignment administrators
- Bitwise administrators
- Comparison administrators
- Execution administrators
- Incrementing/decrementing administrators
- Logical administrators
- String administrators

The operators are recorded as found on http://www.php.net/manual/en/language.operators. php. There are a few operators we're going to talk about so you can get up and running with PHP as fast as could possible. These incorporate a percentage of the throwing administrators that we'll just skim the surface of for the time being. Every operator has four basic properties in addition to its main functionality:

- Operator associativity
- Number of operands
- Order of precedence
- Types of operands

The easiest option to begin is by discussing the operands.

1. Number of Operands

Diverse operands take distinctive quantities of operands. Numerous operators are utilized to join two expressions into a more intricate single expression; these are called *binary operators*. Parallel operators incorporate multiplication, subtraction, addition, and division.

Some operators take one operand; these are called *unary operators*. Consider the negative administrator (-) that multiplies a numeric value by –1. The preincrement what's more, predecrement administrators depicted in Chapter 3 are additionally unary administrators.

A *ternary operator* takes three operands. The shorthand for an if statement, which we'll discuss later when examining conditionals, takes three operands.

2. Types of Operands

You should be aware of the kind of operand on which an administrator is intended to work in light of the fact that certain administrators anticipate that their operands will be of specific data types.

PHP endeavors to make your life as simple as could be expected under the circumstances via consequently changing over operands to the data type that an administrator is anticipating. There are times, nonetheless, that an automatic conversion isn't conceivable.

Mathematical administrators are a case of where you should be watchful with your types. They take just numbers as operands. For instance, when you attempt to multiply two strings, PHP can change over the strings to numbers. While "Becker" * "Furniture" is not a valid expression, it returns zero. Then again, an expression that is changed over without a slip is "70" * "80". This leads to 5600. Though 70 and 80 are strings, PHP has the capacity change them to the number type needed by the mathematical operator. There will be times when you need to expressly set or convert a variable's type.

There are two approaches to do this in PHP: to begin with, by utilizing set type to really change the data type; or second, by casting, which incidentally changes over the value. PHP uses castings to change over data types. At the point when PHP does the casting for you automatically, it's called *implicit casting*. You can likewise indicate data types unequivocally, yet it's not something that you'll likely need to do.

The cast types permitted are:

(int), (integer)

Cast to integer, entire numbers without a decimal part.

(bool), (boolean)

Cast to Boolean.

(float), (twofold), (genuine)

Cast to float, numbers that may include a decimal part.

(string)

Cast to string.

(array)

Cast to array.

(object)

Cast to object.

To utilize a cast, place it before the variable to cast, as evident in example 6.2, the $test_string variable has the string 1234

Sample 6.2. Throwing a variable

```
$test=1234;

$test_string = (string)$test;
```

Remember that it may not be evident what will happen when casting between specific types. You may keep running into difficulties on the off chance that you don't watch yourself at the point when controlling variable types.

Some binary operators, for example, the *assignment operators*, have further confinements on the lefthand operand. Since the *assignment operator* is allocating a quality to the lefthand operator, it must be something that can take a value, for example, a variable.

Sample 6.3. Lefthand expressions

3 = $locations;/awful - a quality can't be doled out to the exacting 3

$a + $b = $c;/awful - the expression on the left isn't one variable

$c = $a + $b;/OK

$stores = "Becker"." ".”Furniture";/OK

There is a less difficult approach to recall this. The lefthand expression in assignment operations is known as an L-value. L-values in PHP are variables, components of an array, and object properties.

Order of Preference

The Order of Preference of an administrator figures out which operator processes first in an expression. For example, the multiplication and division process before addition as well as subtraction. You can see a simplified table at *http://www.zend.com/manual/language.operators.php#language.operators.precedence*

On the off chance that the administrators have the same priority, they are handled in the request they show up in the expression. For instance, multiplication and division prepare in the request in which they show up in an expression in light of the fact that they have the same priority. Administrators with the same priority can happen in any request without influencing the result.

Most expressions don't have more than one administrator of the same priority level, on the other hand the request in which they process doesn't change the outcome. As indicated in Simple 6.4, when adding and subtracting the accompanying succession of numbers, it doesn't make a difference whether you add or subtract first—the outcome is still 1.

PHP has a few levels of priority, enough that it's hard to stay informed concerning them without checking a reference. Table 4-2 is a rundown of PHP administrators sorted by request of priority from most noteworthy to least. Administrators with the same level number are all of the same priority.

Sample 6.4. Order of Preference

2 + 4 - 5 == 1;

4 - 5 + 2 == 1;

4 * 5/2 == 10;

5/2 * 4 == 10;

2 + 4 - 5 == 1;

```
4 - 5 + 2 == 1;
```

When using expressions that contain administrators of diverse priority levels, the order can change the value of the expression. You can utilize parentheses, (and), to override the priority levels or just to make the expression easier to read.

Illustration 6.5 demonstrates to change the default priority.

Illustration 6.5. Changing the default priority using parenthesis

```
echo 2 * 3 + 4 + 1;

echo 2 * (3 + 4 + 1);
```

The result is:

```
11

16
```

In the second expression, the multiplication is done last due to the parenthesis overriding the default priority.

PHP has a few levels of priority, enough that it's hard to keep track without checking a reference.

Associativity

All operators/ administrators process handle their administrators in a certain direction. This direction is called associativity, and it relies on upon the type of administrator. Most administrators are processed from left to right, which is called left associativity. E.g. in the expression 3 + 5 – 2, 3 and 5 are included, and afterward 2 is subtracted from the result, resulting 8. While left associativity implies that the expression is assessed from left to right, right associativity implies the opposite.

Since the assignment operator/administrator has right associativity, it is one of the exemptions since right associativity is less common. The expression $a=$b=$c forms by $b being assigned the estimation of $c, and afterward $a being assigned the value of $b. This assigns a similar value to the majority of the variables. If the assignment administrator is right associative, the variables may not have the same value.

In case you believe that this is unfathomably complicated, don't worry. These principles are implemented only incase that you fail to be clear on your instructions. Remember that you should always use brackets in your expressions to make your real meaning clearer. This helps both PHP and other individuals who may want to read your code.

In the event that you inadvertently utilize & rather than &&, or | rather than ||, you'll wind up misunderstanding the operator. & and | look at twofold information a little bit at a time.

PHP will change over your operands into binary and apply binary operators/administrators.

Relational Operators

In Chapter 3 we look at assignment and math operators. Relation operators give the capacity to look at two operands and return either TRUE or FALSE with respect to the examination. An expression that evaluates just TRUE or FALSE is known as a Boolean expression, which we talked about in the past section. These examinations incorporate tests for equality and less than or greater than. These comparison operators permit you to tell PHP when to do something in view of whether a comparison is genuine so that choices can be made in your code.

Equality

The equality operator/administrators, a double equals sign (==), is utilized as often as possible. Utilizing the single equals sign (=) in its place is a typical mistake in programs, since it allots values rather than testing equality.

In the event that the two operands are equal, TRUE is returned; otherwise, FALSE is returned. In case you're echoing your outcomes, TRUE is printed as 1 in your browser. FALSE is 0 and won't show in your browser.

It's an easy build although it permits you to test for conditions. On the off chance that the operands are of distinctive sorts, PHP endeavors to convert them prior to the comparison.

For instance, “1” == 1 is valid. Additionally, $a == 1 is valid if the variable $a is allocated to 1.

In case you don’t need the equality administrator to automatically convert types, you can utilize the *identity operator*, a triple equals sign (===), which checks whether the results and types are the same. For instance, “1” === 1 is false since they’re different types, because a string is not equal to an integer.

Infrequently you may need to verify whether two things are distinctive. *The inequality operator*, an exclamation mark before the equivalents sign (!=), checks for the opposite of equality, which implies that it is not equivalent to anything; for that reason, it’s FALSE.

“1” != “A”/valid or true

“1” != “1”/false

✓ *Comparison administrators/operators*

You may need to check for more than just equality. Comparison administrators test the relationship between two values. You may be acquainted with these from secondary school math. They incorporate less than (<), less-than or equal to (<=), greater than (>), and greater-than or equal to (>=).

For instance, 3<4 is TRUE, while 3<3 is FALSE, and 3<=3 is TRUE.

Comparison administrators are regularly used to check for something incident up until a set point. E.g. an online store may offer free delivering in case you buy five or more commodities. Therefore, the code must compare the quantity of commodities with the number five before changing the shipping cost.

Logical administrators/operators

Logical administrators work with the Boolean outcomes of logical administrators to construct more complex logical expressions; there are four logical administrators which are additionally Boolean administrators.

To test whether both operands are genuine, use the AND administrator, also written to as the double ampersands (&&). Both the twofold ampersand and AND are logical administrators; the main distinction is that the double ampersand is assessed before the AND administrator. The administrators || as well as OR follow the same principle. TRUE is returned if both operands are TRUE; generally, FALSE is returned.

To test whether one operand is TRUE, use the OR administrator, which is as well written as double vertical bars or pipes (||). Genuine is returned just if either or both operands are TRUE.

Utilizing the OR administrator can bring about tricky program logic issues. In case PHP finds that the first operand is TRUE, it won't assess the second operand. While this spares execution time, you should be cautious that the second administrator doesn't contain code that should be executed for your program to work apprpriately.

To test whether only one operand is TRUE, utilize XOR. XOR returns TRUE if one and one operand is TRUE. It returns FALSE if both operands are TRUE.

To invalidate a Boolean quality, use the NOT administrator, written as an exclamation mark(!). It returns TRUE if the operand has an value of FALSE. It returns FALSE if the operand is TRUE.

Conditionals

Conditionals, like variables, form a building block in our establishment of PHP development.

They change a script's process as indicated by the criteria set in the code. There are three essential conditionals in PHP:

- if
- ? : (shorthand for an if articulation)
- switch

The switch statement is helpful when you have various things you need to do and need to take diverse activities based on the contents of a variable. The switch statement is examined in more detail later in this section.

The if Statement

The if statement offers the ability to execute a piece of code if the supplied condition is TRUE; generally, the code block doesn't execute. The condition can be any expression, including tests for nonzero, equality, null, variables, and returned qualities from capacities.

Regardless, each and every conditional you make incorporates a restrictive clause. In the event that a condition is TRUE, the code block in curly braces ({}) is executed. If not, PHP overlooks it and moves to the second condition, proceeding through all provisions composed until PHP hits an else. At that point, it consequently executes that block just if the IF condition turns out to be FALSE; else, it proceeds onward. The curly braces are not required if you have one line of code to execute in the block. An else explanation is most certainly not continuously needed.

The else block dependably needs to come last and be dealt with as though it's the default activity. This is like the semicolon (;). Regular true conditions are:

- $var, if $var has a quality other than the empty set (0), an empty string, or NULL
- isset ($var), if $var has any quality other than NULL, including the empty set or an empty string
- TRUE or any variation thereof

We haven't discussed about the second bullet point. isset( ) is a function that checks whether a variable is *set*. A set variable has a value other than NULL.

The syntax for the **if** statement is:

```
if (conditional expression){
piece of code;
}
```

If the expression in the conditional block assesses to TRUE, the block of code that tails it executes. In this case, if the variable $username is set to 'Administrator', a welcome message is printed. If not, nothing happens.

```
if ($username == "Administrator") {
echo ('Welcome to the administrator page.');
}
```

The curly braces aren't required if you need to execute stand out statement, yet it's great practice to dependably utilize them, as it makes the code simpler to read and harderer to change.

The else statement

The optional else statement gives a default piece of code that executes if the condition returned is FALSE. else can't be utilized without an if statement, as it doesn't take a conditional itself. Therefore, else and if need to always be together in your code.

Remember to finish off the code block from the if conditional when you've used props to begin your piece of code. Like the if block, the else block ought to as well use curvy braces to start and end the code.

The elseif statement

Most of the above is incredible with the exception of when you need to test for a few conditions at the same time.

To do this, you can utilize the elseif statement. It takes into account testing of extra conditions until one is discovered to be true or until you hit the else block. Each elseif has its own code hinder that comes specifically after the elseif condition. The elseif must come after the if statement and before an else statement if one exists.

Case 6.7. Checking various conditions

```
if ($username == "Admin"){

echo ('Welcome to the administrator page.');

}

elseif ($username == "Guest"){

echo ('Please investigate around.');

}

else {

echo ("Welcome back, $username.");

}
```

Here you can check for two conditions and take different activities in light of each of the qualities for $username. At that point you additionally have the alternative to do something else if the $username isn't one of the initial two.

The next construct develops on the ideas of the if/else statement, yet it permits you to effectively check the results of an expression to numerous qualities without having a different if/else for every value.

The ? Operator

The ?operator is a ternary operator, which implies it takes three operands. It meets expectations like an if statement however gives back a value from one of the two expressions. The conditional expression decides the value of the expression. A colon (:) is utilized to separate the expressions, as indicated here:

```
{expression} ? return_when_expression_true : return_
when_expression_false;
```

Case 4.8. Utilizing the ? operator to make a message

```
<?php

$logged_in = TRUE;

$user = "Administrator";

$banner = ($logged_in==TRUE)?"Welcome back,
$user!":"Please login.";

echo "$banner";

?>
```

The above example 4.8 produces

Welcome back, Admin!

This can be really helpful for checking for errors. However, we should take a gander at a statement that lets you check an expression against a list of possible values to pick the executable code.

The switch Statement

The switch statement compares an expression with various values. It's really common to have an expression such as a variable, for which you'll need to execute different code for every value stored in the variable. Case in point, you may have a variable called $action, which may have the values add, modify, and delete. The switch statement makes it simple to characterize a square of code to execute in light of each of those values. To show the difference between using the if statement and the switch statement to test a variable for a few qualities, we'll reveal to you the code for the if statement (in illustration 6.9) and hat for the switch statement (in example 6.10)

Illustration 6.9. Utilizing if to test for various qualities

```
if ($action == "Include") {

echo "Perform activities for including.";

echo "The greatest number of statements as you like
can be in every square.";

}
```

```
elseif ($action == "MODIFY") {
echo "Perform activities for modifying.";
}
elseif ($action == "Erase") {
echo "Perform activities for erasing.";
}
```

Case 6.10. Utilizing switch to test for various qualities

```
switch ($action) {
case "Include":
echo "Perform activities for including.";
echo "The greatest number of statements as you like can be in every piece.";
break;
case "MODIFY":
echo "Perform activities for modifying.";
break;
case "Erase":
echo "Perform activities for erasing.";
break;
}
```

The switch statement lives up to expectations by taking the value after the switch keyword and comparing it to the cases in the order in which they are arranged. If no case matches, the code isn't executed. When a case matches, the code is executed. The code in consequent cases additionally executes until the end of the switch statement or until a break keyword. This is helpful for procedures that have chronological steps. If the client had done several steps, he can resume the process where he left off.

The expression after the switch statement must assess to a simple type e.g. an integer, a string or a number. An array can be utilized just if a specific individual from the cluster is referenced as a simple type.

There are various approaches to direct PHP not to execute cases other than the matching case.

6.3 Breaking Out

If you need just the code in the matching block to execute, place a break keyword at the end of that block. At the point when PHP goes over the break pivotal word, processing jumps to the following line after the whole switch statement. Case 6.11 outlines how processing works to expectations with no break statements.

Case 6.11. What happens when there are no break keywords

$action = “ASSEMBLE ORDER”;

```
switch ($action) {
case " ASSEMBLE ORDER":
echo "Perform activities for order assembly.<br/>";
case "PACKAGE":
echo "Perform activities for packing.<br/>";
case "SHIP":
echo "Perform activities for shipping.<br/>";
}
```

If the value of $action is "ASSEMBLE ORDER", the outcome is:

Perform activities for order assembly.

Perform activities for packing.

Perform activities for shipping.

On the other hand, if a client has assembled an order, an estimation of "PACKAGE" produces these:

Perform activities for packaging.

Perform activities for shipping.

Defaulting

The SWITCH statement likewise gives an approach to do something if none of alternative cases match, which is the same as the else statement in an if, elseif, or else block.

Use the DEFAULT: statement for the SWITCH's last case statement (see Example 4-12).

Example 4-12. Using the DEFAULT: statement to produce a error

```
switch ($action) {
case "ADD":
echo "Perform activities for addding.";
break;
case "MODIFY":
echo "Perform activities for modifying.";
break;
case "DELETE":
echo "Perform activities for deleting.";
break;
default:
echo "Slip: Action must be either ADD, MODIFY, or DELETE.";
}
```

The switch statement additionally bolsters the alternate syntax in which the switch and endswitch essential words characterize the beginning and end of the switch rather than the curly braces {}, as indicated in Example 6.13.

Example 6.13. Utilizing endswitch to end the switch definition

```
switch ($action):
case “ADD”:
echo “Perform actions for adding.”;
break;
case “MODIFY”:
echo “Perform actions for modifying.”;
break;
case “DELETE”:
echo “Perform actions for deleting.”;
break;
default:
echo “Error: Action must be either ADD, MODIFY, or DELETE.”;
endswitch;
```

You’ve discovered that you can have your programs execute different code subject to conditions called expressions. The switch statement gives a suitable format to checking the value of an expression against various possible values.

6.4 Looping

Since you've changed the stream of your PHP program based on examinations, you need to realize that if you need to rehash an assignment until an examination is FALSE, you'll need to use LOOPING. Every time the code loop executes, it is called *iteration*. This is valuable for some basic errands e.g. showing the outcomes of a query by loopng through the returned columns. PHP gives the while, for, and do ... while develops to perform loops.

Each of the loop developments needs two fundamental bits of data. To begin with, the condition to stop looping is characterized simply like the comparison in an if statement. Second, the code to perform likewise obliged and specified either on a single line or inside curly braces. A logical mistake would be to exclude the code from a loop that depends on the code executed to bring about the circle to quit, creating an infinite loop.

You've discovered that you can have your projects execute different code in light of conditions called expressions. The switch statement gives an advantageous arrangement to checking the estimation of an expression against various conceivable qualities.

The code is executed the length of the expression assesses to TRUE. To dodge an infinite loop, which would loop eternally, your code ought to have the expressions in the end become FALSE. When such a situation happens, the loop stops and execution proceeds to the next line of code, taking after the logical loop.

while Loops

The while loop takes the expression followed by the code to execute.

The syntax for some a while loop is:

```
while (expression)

{

code to execute;

}
```

A sample is demonstrated in Example 6.14.

Sample 4-14. An example while circle that checks to 10

```
<?php

$num = 1;

while ($num <= 10){

print “Number is $num<br/>”;

$num++;

}

print ‘Done.’;

?>
```

Sample 4-14 produces these:

Number is 1

Number is 2

Number is 3

Number is 4

Number is 5

Number is 6

Number is 7

Number is 8

Number is 9

Number is 10

Done.

Prior to the circle starts, the variable $num is set to 1. This is called instating a counter variable. Every time the code square executes, it expands the worth in $num by 1 with the statement $num++;. After 10 iterations, the assessment $num <= 10 gets to be FALSE, then the loop stops and it prints Done. Remember to expand the $num var, as the while loop relies on upon it. Be cautious so as not to make an infinite loop. It has the undesirable impact of not giving back your page and taking a ton of processing time on the web server.

do ... while Loops

The do ... while loop takes an expression such as a while statement though it puts it at the end. The syntax is:

```
do {
code to execute;
} while (expression);
```

This circle is helpful when you need to execute a piece of code at any rate once despite of the expression value. E.g. let's check to 10 with this loop, as indicated in Illustration 6.15.

Illustration 6.15. Numbering to 10 with do … while

```
<?php
$num = 1;
do {
echo "Number is ".$num."<br/>";
$num++;
} while ($num <= 10);
echo "Done.";
?>
```

Case 6.15 creates the same results as Example 6.14; if you change the estimation of

$num to 11, the loop forms differently:

```
<?php
$num = 11;
do {
echo $num;
$num++;
} while ($num <= 10);
?>
```

This produces:

11

The code on the loop displays 11 given that the loop dependably executes at least once. Taking after the pass, while evaluates to FALSE, making execution to drop out of the do…while loop.

for Loops

for loops give the same general functionality as while loops though they require a predefined area for introducing and changing a counter value.

Their syntax is: for (iniitialization expression; condition expression; modification expression){code that is executed;

}

A n example for loop is:

```
<?php
```

```
for ($num = 1; $num <= 10; $num++) {
print "Number is $num<br/>\n";
}
?>
```

This produces:

Number is 1

Number is 2

Number is 3

Number is 4

Number is 5

Number is 6

Number is 7

Number is 8

Number is 9

Number is 10

At the point when your PHP program process the for loop, the initialization segment is assessed.

For every iteration of the part of code that increments, the counter executes furthermore, is trailed by a check to verify whether you're finished. The outcome is an a more conservative and easy-to-read statement.

At the point when specifying you're for loop, if you

would prefer not to incorporate one of the expressions such as the introduction expression, you may preclude it, yet you must incorporate the isolating semicolons (;). Sample 4-16 demonstrates the use of a for loop without the initialization expression.

Breaking Out of a Loop

PHP gives something similar to an emergency stop button for a loop : the break statement.

Ordinarily, the main way out of a loop is to fulfill the expression that decides at the point when to stop the loop. If the code on the loop finds an error that makes proceeding with the circle pointless or unimaginable, you can break out of the loop on by using the break statement. It's similar to getting your shoelace stuck in an escalator. It truly doesn't bode well for the lift to continue moving! However, those old ones did!

Conceivable issues you may experience in a loop consist of coming up short on space when you're writing a document or aiming to divide by zero. In Example 6.16, we reenact what can happen if you divide based an obscure entry instated from submission of a form (that could be a client supplied value). If your client is malignant or just plain careless, she may enter a negative value where you're expecting a positive value (in spite of the fact that this ought to be gotten in your form validation process). In the code that is executed as a fraction of the loop, the code checks to verify the

$counter is not equivalent to zero. If it is, the code calls break.

Sample 6.16. Using break to evade division by zero

```
<?php
$counter = - 3;
for(; $counter < 10; $counter++){
/Check for division by zero
if ($counter == 0){
echo "Stopping to avoid division by zero.";
break;
}
echo "100/$counter<br/>";
}
?>
```

This results in the following:

100/–3

100/–2

100/–1

Stopping to avoid division by zero.

Obviously, there may be times when you would prefer not to simply skip one execution of the loop code. The continue statement performs this for you.

Continue Statements

You can utilize continue statement to impede processing the present block of code in a circle and bounce to the following emphasis of the circle. It's different from break in that it doesn't quit handling the circle totally. You're essentially skipping ahead to the following emphasis. Verify you are modifying your test variable before the continue statement, otherwise, an infinite loop is possible. Case 6.17 demonstrates the former sample utilizing continue rather than break.

Case 6.16. Using continue instead of break

```
<?php
$counter = - 3;
for (; $counter < 10; $counter++){
/Check for division by zero
<?php
$counter=-3;
for (;$counter<10;$counter++){
//check for division by zero
if ($counter==0){
echo "Skipping to avoid division by zero.<br>";
continue;
```

```
}
echo "100/$counter ",100/$counter,"<br />";
}
?>
```

The new output is like in the following sequence:

100/ - 3 - 33.3333333333

100/ - 2 - 50

100/ - 1 - 100

Skipping to maintain a strategic distance from division by zero

100/1 100

100/2 50

100/3 33.3333333333

100/4 25

100/5 20

100/6 16.6666666667

100/7 14.2857142857

100/8 12.5

100/9 11.1111111111

Notice that the loop skipped the $counter value of zero and it regardless proceeded with the next value.

We've now gone through the majority of the major program flow language constructs. We've talked about the building blocks for controlling program flow in your programs. Expressions can be as direct as TRUE or FALSE or as mind boggling as relational comparison with local operators. The expressions consolidated with program flow construct develops like the if statement and switch makes decision-making simple.

We additionally examined while, do ... while, and for loops. Loops are extremely helpful for basic element web page tasks such as showing the outcomes from a query in an HTML table.

CHAPTER 7

FUNCTIONS

To compose PHP programs that contain more than only a few pages of code and are still systematized well enough to be valuable, you have to have an in-depth understanding of *functions*. Functions let you dispose of rehashing the same lines of code again and again in your programs. Functions work by allocating a name called a function name to a lump of code. Subsequently, you execute the code by calling that name. There are many inherent functions in PHP. For instance, print_r is a function that prints coherent data around a variable in plain English as opposed to code. If given a string, whole number, or float, the quality itself is printed with the print_r function. If given an array, qualities are demonstrated as keys and components. A similar format is utilized for objects. In PHP 5.0, print_r and var_export show secured and private properties of objects.

Functions run the array from aggregate_info to imap_ping through pdf_open_image. Since there are many of them, we can just cover a few fundamentals in this chapter, although we'll give you enough data that you'll be using functions like an expert as a in a very short time.

You can look http://www.php.net for a thorough list of functions.

Specifically, we'll go over the following:

- How to make a function, give it a name, and execute that function
- How to send values to a function and utilize them in the function
- How to return values from a function and apply them in your code
- How to verify that a function exists before you attempt using it

The point of coding when you may split code into a function is a somewhat of a subjective judgment call. Unquestionably, if you discover yourself rehashing a few lines of code again and again, it bodes well to pull that code into its own function. That will make your code simpler to read as well as protect you from having to make numerous improvements if you choose to do something else with that piece of code, as its then in only one spot, not various spots where you'd need to search and replace to change it.

A function is a block of code that allows values, forms them, and afterward performs an action. Consider making cakes and baking them in a oven as a function. You put the raw dough into the oven, which makes the dough mixture the input. The oven then bakes the dough mixture; this is the function. The outcome of the function for baking the cakes is the edible, baked cakes. The function may even take other inputs, for example, temperature and baking time. These different inputs are called *parameters*.

Parameters send data to a function, and afterward the function executes the code. Functions can use anywhere in the range of zero parameters to an entire list. In Illustration 7.1, you'll utilize the echo function to show some text. echo shows message that you send to it as a parameter. Most functions need you to put their parameters within parentheses, yet echo is a special case to this idea. Echoing of all variables is about fool-proof! Figure 7.1 shows how the outcome of the script shows up in a program.

Illustration 7.1. The pervasive Hello world!

```
<?php
echo (“Hello world !”);
?>
```

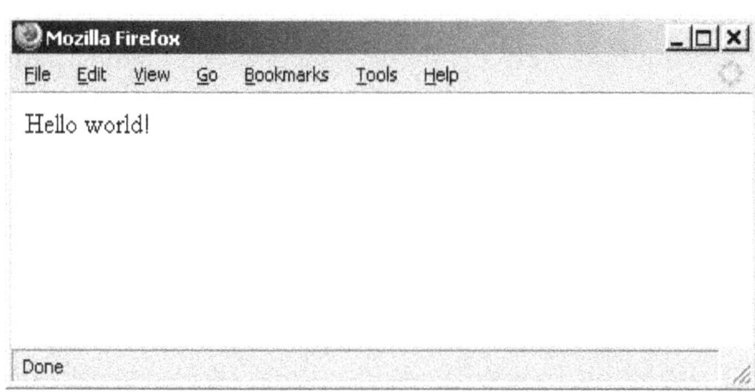

How the echo output looks in the browser window

The echo function basically sends on the "Welcome world!" string to the program/browser once you load the PHP document. echo is in fact a PHP language construct. Basically, this means it has the capacity to work without encasing its parameters in parentheses. It's important to note that true functions need parentheses in most cases.

You can use one of PHP's numerous inherent functions or identify your own. We'll talk all the more about identifying different functions later in this part.

7.1 Calling Functions

Functions that are incorporated into PHP can be called from any PHP script. When you call functions, you are executing the code inside them, aside from the code is reusable and more retainable. One inherent function, indicated in Example 7.2, is *phpinfo*. It returns technical and configuration data about your PHP installation.

The function helps you to analyze basic issues and problems. You may find that this is amongst the best places to look when verifying whether you meet the prerequisites of a PHP script. Figure 7.2 shows just piece of the data contained on this page. If a function call doesn't work, this page aide in analyzing whether PHP has been assembled with the essential modules. Try not to leave a script using phpinfo( ): on a production web server, although, in light of the fact that it reveals data about your server that could be utilized by hackers for pernicious agenda/intentions.

To call a function, write the name of the function, an opening parenthesis ((), the parameters, an end parenthesis ()), and after that a semicolon (;). It would resemble this: *function_name(parameters);*. Function names aren't case-sensitive, so calling phpinfo is the same as calling PhpInfo. As indicated in Example 7.3, this is what calling a function resembles: md5($mystring);.

Most functions have return values that you'll either use in an examination or store in a variable. An incredible place to begin is the md5 function. md5 is a one-way hash function which is like a checksum used to verify the reliability of a string. md5 changes a message into a rigid series of digits, called a *message digest*. You can then perform a *hashcheck*, comparing the computed message digest against a message digest decoded with a public key to verify that the message was not interfered with.

Sample 5.3 makes a 128-bit long md5 mark of the string "mystring".

Case 5.3 shows the following outcome:

169319501261c644a58610f967e8f9d0

The return value, which is analyzed comprehensively in this section, is allocated to the variable $signature, which then shows/displays the output.

Case 7.2. Showing data about the PHP sorrounding

```
<?php
phpinfo( );
?>
```

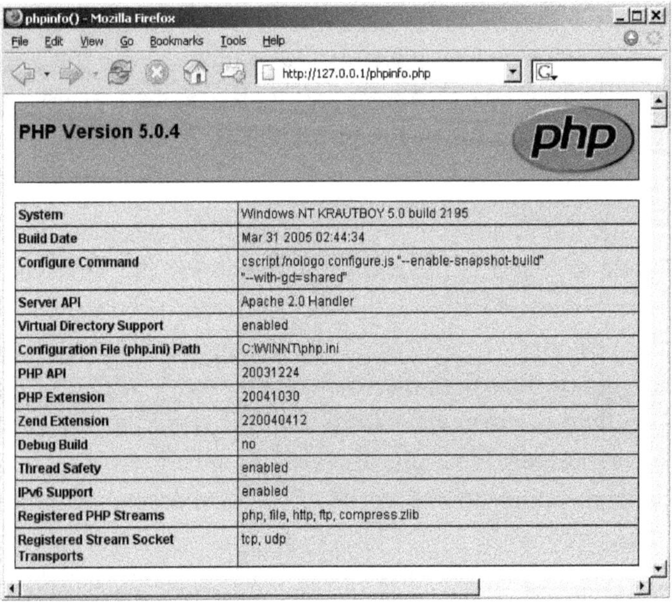
phpinfo() - Mozilla Firefox
File Edit View Go Bookmarks Tools Help
http://127.0.0.1/phpinfo.php
PHP Version 5.0.4
php
System | Windows NT KRAUTBOY 5.0 build 2195
Build Date | Mar 31 2005 02:44:34
Configure Command | cscript /nologo configure.js "--enable-snapshot-build" "--with-gd=shared"
Server API | Apache 2.0 Handler
Virtual Directory Support | enabled
Configuration File (php.ini) Path | C:\WINNT\php.ini
PHP API | 20031224
PHP Extension | 20041030
Zend Extension | 220040412
Debug Build | no
Thread Safety | enabled
IPv6 Support | enabled
Registered PHP Streams | php, file, http, ftp, compress.zlib
Registered Stream Socket Transports | tcp, udp

Figure 7.2. Information about PHP displayed in the browser

A typical use for md5 is to verify that a document/file didn't get to be degenerated while it was being transferred. The document and its md5 mark are analyzed after their reaching the receiver. If they match, you realize that it's impossible that the document's content were tampered with during the process of their transfer.

If they're different, you realize that the document is degenerate or corrupt.

This illustration shows how you can perform a perplexing procedure using a function without needing to stress over how that procedure really does it. This is the genuine power of functions.

7.2 Defining Functions

There are as of now numerous functions incorporated into PHP. Nonetheless, you can identify your own also, break down your code into functions. To identify your own functions, begin with the function statement:

function some_function([arguments]) { code to execute; }

The sections ([ ]) mean optional. The code could likewise be composed with *optional_ arguments* instead of [arguments]. The function key word is accompanied by the function name. Function names comply with the same principles as other named objects e.g. variables, in PHP. One pair of parenthesis (()) must come next. If your function has parameters, they're specified inside of the parentheses. Lastly, the code to execute is recorded between curly braces, as shown in the past code illustration.

You can identify/define functions at any point in your code and call them from virtually anywhere.

The rules of this scope are portrayed in Chapter 3. As

you may recall, the *scope* of a variable is the setting inside which it's defined. Generally, all PHP variables have just one scope. A single scope compasses included and all necessary files as well. The function is defined on the same file or included in an incorporated document file. Functions can have parameters and return values that permit you to reuse code.

To make your own function that easily shows a different hello message, you would compose it as follows:

```
<?php
function hi( )
{
echo ("Hello from function-land!");
}
/Call the function
hi( );
?>
```

this shows as:

Hello from function-land!

The hi function doesn't take any parameters, so you don't list anything between the parentheses. Since you've defined a basic function, how about we blend in a few parameters?

Parameters

Parameters give a helpful approach to pass data to a function when you call it without needing to stress over variable scope. In PHP, you don't need to characterize what kind of information a parameter holds—only the parameters' names need to be specified.

A sample of a function that takes a parameter is *strtolower*, which changes over your string "Hi world!" to lowercase. It takes a parameter of the sort string, which is a data type depicted in Chapter 3. Additionally, there's another function called *strtoupper* which changes over all characters of your string into capitalized letters, as demonstrated in Example 7.4.

Sample 7.4. Utilizing the string capitalization functions inside of another function that takes a parameter

```
<?php

/Capitalize a string function underwrite( $str )

{

/First, change over all characters to lowercase

$str = strtolower($str);

/Second, change over the first character to capitalized

$str{0} = strtoupper($str{0});/$str{0] gets to the first character in the string

echo $str;

}
```

```
capitalize("hEllo WoRld!" );

?>
```

Case 7.4 yields the accompanying:

Hi world!

The value of $str was echoed inside the function on the grounds that you didn't specify any way to get the value out of the function. As noted above, $str{0} gets to the first character in a string.

PHP doesn't need you to characterize whether a function really returns a value, or what data type it returns.

Parameters can likewise contain default values. With a default value, you really don't need to pass the function any info for it to set the default. How about we change your uppercase function to have a default value that permits you to capitalize the first letter of every word or simply the entire sentence? We're doing this in Example 7.5.

Illustration 7.5. Making an uppercase function with a default parameter $each

```
<?php

/Capitalize a string or just the first letter of every word
function underwrite( $str, $each=TRUE ) {

/First, change over all characters to lowercase or non-first-word letters may remain capitalized
```

```
$str = strtolower($str);
if ($each === TRUE) {
$str = ucwords ($str);
} else {
$str = strtoupper($str);
}
echo ("$str <br/>");
}
capitalize("hEllo WoRld!");
echo ("Now do the same with the echo parameter set to FALSE.<br>");
capitalize("hEllo WoRld!",FALSE);
?>
```

This results in the following:

Hello World!

Now do the same with the echo parameter set to FALSE

HELLO WORLD!

Parameter References

When you pass a query to the function, a local duplicate is made in the function to store the value. Any progressions made to that value influence just the local duplicate of the variable in the function, not the origin of the parameter. You can define parameters that modify the source variable by defining reference parameters.

Reference parameters define references by putting an ampersand (&) right before the parameter in the function's definition. We should modify the capitalize function from Example 7.5 to take a reference variable for the string to capitalize, which is indicated in Example 7.6.

Illustration 7.6 Modifying capitalize ( ) to take a reference parameter

```
<?php
function capitalize ( &$str, $each=TRUE ){
{/First, change over all characters to lowercase
$str = strtolower($str);
if ($each === genuine) {
$str = ucwords($str);
} else {
$str{0} = strtoupper($str{0});
}
}
$str = "Hi WoRld!";
underwrite( $str );
```

```
echo $str;
?>
```

Example 7.8 produces the following:

Hello World!

Since capitalize defined the $str parameter as a source of perspective parameter, a connection to the source variable was sent to the function when it was executed. The function basically accessed and modified the source variable. Had the variable not been announced as reference, the first estimation of “hEllo WoRld!” would have shown.

Including and Requiring PHP Files

To make your code easier to read, you can put your functions in a different file.

Numerous PHP add-ons that you download off the Internet contain functions which have been put into the records by now that you basically include in your PHP program. On the other hand, PHP gives four functions that empower you to embed code from different files:

- incorporate
- require
- include_once
- require_once

Each and every one of the include and require functions

take a local doc as input. Require and include functions are quite similar in their functionality aside irrespective the way in which they handle a resource which cannot be retrieved. For instance, *include* and *include_once* give a notice if the resource isn't retrievable and tries to proceed with execution of the program. The *require* and *require_once* functions give stop preparing of the specific page if they can't recover the resource. Presently we're going to get more specific about these four functions.

- ✓ **The include Statement**

The include statement permits you to incorporate and join other PHP scripts to your own script. You can consider it just taking the included record and embedding it into your PHP document. Case 7.7 is called *add.php*.

Illustration 7.7. A sample include document called add.php

```
<?php
function include( $x, $y ){
return $x + $y;
}
?>
```

Illustration 7.8 presumes that add.php is in the same directory as the script.

Illustration 7.8. Utilizing the include function

```
<?php
include('add.php');
echo add(2, 2);
?>
```

After being executed, this produces:

```
4
```

As clear from example 7.8, the include statement appends other PHP scripts so that you can get to different variables, functions, and classes.

You can name your include records anything you like, however you ought to continuously use the .php extension given that if you name them something else, for example, .inc, it's impossible that a client can ask for the .inc record and the web server will give back the code stored in it. This is a security hazard, as it may expose passwords or insights about how your system functions that can expose shortcomings in your code. This is on the grounds that the PHP interpreter parses just records marked plainly as PHP.

- ✓ **The include_once statement**

A problem may occur when you include numerous hosted PHP scripts as the include statement doesn't check for scripts that have previously been included.

For instance, if you did this:

```
<?php include('add.php');include('add.php');
echo add(2, 2);
?>
```

You'd get this error:

Fatal error: Cannot redeclare add( ) (already declared in /home/www/htmlkb/oreilly/ch5/add.php:2) in/home/www/htmlkb/oreilly/ch5/add.php on line 2

This registry may not be the place your file is found; your record will go wherever you've assigned a spot for it. To evade this kind of mistake/error, you ought to use the include_once statement.

Example 7.9 illustrates the include_once statement.

Example 7.9. Utilizing include_once to include a record

```
<?php
include_once('add.php');
include_once('add.php');
echo add(2, 2);
?>
```

When executed, the output for the following is:

```
4
```

- ✓ **require and require_once functions**

To verify that a record is included and to stop your program if it isn't, use *require* as well as its corresponding item, *require_once*. These are precisely the same as *include* and *include_once* with the exception of that they verify that the document is available; if not, the PHP script's execution is stopped, which wouldn't be a pleasant thing! You ought to use require rather than include if the record you're including defines either basic functions that your script won't have the capacity to execute, or variable definitions, for example, database association details.

For instance, if you endeavor to requirea file that doesn't exist, as follows:

```
<?php
require_once('add_wrong.php');
echo add(2, 2);
?>
```

you'd get this error:

Warning: main(add_wrong.php): neglected to open stream: No such file or directory in/home/www/htmlkb/oreilly/ch5/require_once.php on line 2

Fata error: main( ): Failed opening obliged "add_wrong.php"

The last point we'll cover with functions is the way to test whether a function has been defined before trying to use it.

Testing a Function

If compatibility with different PHP versions is particularly essential to your script, it's important to have the capacity to check for the presence of functions. The function *function_* exists does exactly what you'd anticipate. It takes a string with a function's name and returns TRUE or FALSE depending on whether the function has been defined. For instance, these code tests a function:

```
<?php
$test=function_exists("test_this");
if ($test == TRUE)
{
echo "Function test_this exists.";
}
else
{
echo "Function test_this does not exist.";
/call_different_function( );
}
?>
```

This code displays this statement:

Function test_this does not exist.

The Function test_this does not exist message shows as you haven't defined the function test_this.

You've figured out how to define functions and their parameters and how to pass data forward and backward from them; besides, we've given you some great samples of the most effective method to investigate potential function troubles.

Next, we'll present a substitute style of programming called Object-Oriented (OO) programming. PHP 5.0 has a completely developed OO interface. There is constant debate on which type of coding is better, and in fact, none is better or more worse than the other; it's basically a style issue alongside personal experience.

7.3 Object-Oriented Programming

Object-Oriented programming takes after the same objectives that we examined when discussing functions, basically to make reusing code simpler. It uses classes to group functions and variables together as an object. It may help to consider objects as little secret boxes that can work without you knowing the exact way of how it's done.

Despite everything, they utilize functions; however they get another name when defined in classes. These are called *methods*. The class works as an outline for making objects of the class defined type. Variables can as well be defined in methods; however they pick up the new capacity to be characterized as a major aspect of the class itself.

At the point when another object is made from a class, it is called an *instance* of that class. Any variables that are defined in the class get separate storage space in every occurrence. The separate storage for variables gives the case of an object with the capacity to remember information between method executions.

If you're new to the idea of OO programming, don't panic over getting to understand everything immediately. We'll work with a class in Chapter 8, so it's adequate just to know how to call the techniques. Actually, anything that should be possible with objects should be possible with plain functions. It's simply a matter of style and individual preference.

Creating a Class

Classes are commonly stored in independent documents for reuse. Let's build an object called Cat that has three methods: meow, eat, and purr. The class build defines a class and its name. Class names take after the same naming principles as variables and functions. The code that makes up the class is put between curly braces. The following example makes the Cat class without d or defining any methods variables. You can do a speedy verification of whether the class has been defined, as Example 7.10 illustrates.

Example 7.10. Making an object from the Cat class

```
<?php
class Cat {
}
$fluffy = new Cat( );
echo "Cushy is another ".gettype($fluffy)."!";
?>
```

The above code displays as follows:

Fluffy is a new object!

Creating an Instance

Example 7.10 characterizes the class as well as makes an instance of it. The new keyword advises PHP to give back another example of the Cat class. In spite of the fact that the class doesn't do anything, you can tell that it's characterized as an object. The class is an outline for building occasions. The class specifies what is incorporated in each new example of that class. Every occasion can do everything the class defines inside of the context of the occasion.

Methods and Constructors

Methods are the functions characterized inside of the class. They work inside of nature of the class, including its variables. For classes, there is an exceptional method called a *constructor* that is called when another occurrence of a class is made to do any work that initializes the class, for example, setting up the estimations of variables in the class. The constructor is characterized by making a technique that has the same name as the class, as demonstrated in Example 7.11.

Illustration 7.11. Making the Cat constructor

```
<?php
class Cat {
/Constructor
function Cat( ) {
}
}
?>
```

PHP 5.0 backs syntaxfor making a constructor strategy utilizing _ _constructor, as demonstrated in Example 7.12. If a class in PHP 5.0 doesn't have this system, the old style of using the class name as the system name is used.

Illustration 7.12. Utilizing the PHP 5 style constructor

```
<?php
class Cat {
/Constructor
Function __constructor( ){
}
```

```
}
?>
```

The constructor might likewise contain parameters like whatever other method. Additionally, classes can contain user-defining methods. For the Cat class, you can characterize meow, eat and purr as indicated in Example 7.13.

Example 7.13. Defining three member functions for Cat

```
<?php
Class Cat {
/Constructor
function __constructor( ) {
}
/The cat meows
function meow( ) {
echo “Meow...”;
}
/The cat eats
function eat( ) {
echo “*eats*”;
}
```

```
/The cats purrs
function murmur( ) {
echo "*Purr...*";
}
}
?>
```

When you pronounce another occasion of a class, the client characterized constructor is dependably called, accepting that one exists. As you probably are aware, a class gives the diagram to objects. You make an object from a class. If you see the expression "instantiating a class," this implies the same thing as making an object; consequently, you can consider them as being synonymous. When you make an object, you are making an occasion of a class, which implies you are instantiating a class.

The new build instantiates a class by allocating memory for that new object, which implies that it needs a solitary postfix contention, which is a call to a constructor.

The name of the constructor gives the name of the class to instantiate, and the constructor introduces the new object.

The new construct sends back a reference to the object that was made. This reference is commonly assigned to a variable. Nonetheless, if the reference is not assigned to a variable, the object is inaccessible after the statement in which the new operator completes the process of executing. Illustration 7.14 demonstrates to you generally accepted methods to utilize *new* effectively.

Illustration 7.14. Making another object and assigning it to a variable

```
<?php
Class Cat {
/Constructor
function __constructor( ) {
}
/The cat meows
function meow( ) {
echo "Meow...";
}
/The cat eats
function eat( ) {
echo "*eats*";
}
/The cat purrs
function purr( ) {
echo "*Purr...*";
```

```
}
}
/Assign the new Cat object reference to $myCat
$myCat=new Cat;
?>
```

Variable Scope Within Classes

Classes may contain variables that help in defining their structure and how they are used. Variables inside a class are declared with the var statement. The var statement announces a variable to have *class scope*. Class scope means they're instantly recognizable with any techniques for the class and can be referenced outside the class utilizing a special construct. Example 7.15 adds the $age variable to the Cat class.

Illustration 5-15. Adding the $age variable to Cat

```
<?php
class Cat {
/How old the cat is
var $age;
/PHP 5 uses:
/public $age;
}
?>
```

Whilst referring to techniques and variables from within the class, you must utilize the syntax:

$this->variable or technique name;

The uncommon variable $this always points to the existing executing object.

In Example 7.16, the this-> operator is used to modify the estimation of $age.

Illustration 5-16. Getting to the $age variable using this->

```
<?php
class Cat {
/How old the cat is
var $age;
/Constructor
function Cat($new_age){
/Set the age of this cat to the new age
$this->age = $new_age;
}
/The birthday method increments the age variable
function Birthday( ){
$this->age++;
}
```

```
}
/Create a new instance of the cat object that is one year old
$fluffy = new Cat(1);
echo “Age is $fluffy->age <br/>”;
echo “Birthday<br/>”;
/Increase fluffy’s age
$fluffy->Birthday( );
echo “Age is $fluffy->age <br/>”;
?>
```

Illustration 7.16 creates the following:

Age is 1

Birthday

Age is 2

Note that you can get to the estimation of $age from outside the class by utilizing the name of the class with the - > operator rather than this.

Inheritance

When asserting classes, it’s likewise feasible to isolate functionality into subclasses that naturally inherit the systems and variables of the class on which they are based. This can be helpful if you’re adding functionality to a class without modifying the original class. Example 7.17 shows how properties and techniques are acquired from the parent class for the *Domestic_Cat class.*

The extends operator

When a class inherits from another class, the class from which it acquires properties is known as the *superclass*. When announcing a subclass, use the extends keyword to specify from which class it's inheriting. Case 7.17 demonstrates an illustration of this.

Case 7.17. Using extends keywords to define a subclass

```
<?php
class Cat {
/How old the cat is
var $age;
function Cat($new_age){
/Set the age of this cat to the new age
$this->age = $new_age;
}
function Birthday( ){
$this->age++;
}
}
```

```
class Domestic_Cat expands Cat {
/Constructor
function Domestic_Cat( ) {
}
/Sleep like a domestic cat
function sleep( ) {
echo("Zzzzzz.<br/>");
}
}
$fluffy=new Domestic_Cat( );
$fluffy->Birthday( );
$fluffy->sleep( );
echo "Age is $fluffy->age <br/>";
?>
```

Case 7.17 outputs the following:

> Zzzzzz.
>
> Age is 1

Notice that you can access the Birthday function from the Cat class and the recently defined sleep method despite of which level in the object defined the method.

The parent operator

A Domestic_Cat is a Cat in all regards. However, it contains the base methods for a Cat. It's likewise feasible to override existing functionality from the superclass to give your own new code. You just reclassify the function in the new class.

When expanding classes to override functions in your class that are now defined in the superclass, you can still execute the code from the parent class and after that include your own particular functionality. To call the parent class technique before your code, use:

parent::method_from_parent

This calls the parent system in the superclass. You can then add it to your code, as shown in Example 7.18.

Illustration 7.18. Utilizing the parent build

```
<?php
class Cat {
/How old the cat is
var $age;
function Cat($new_age){
/Set the age of this cat to the new age
$this->age = $new_age;
}
```

```
function Birthday( ){
$this->age++;
}
function Eat( ){
echo "chomp chomp.";
}
function Meow( ){
echo "meow.";
}
}
class Domestic_Cat extends Cat {
/Constructor
function Domestic_Cat( ) {
}
```

Static Methods and Variables

Methods and variables can likewise be utilized and accessed if they are defined as static in a class. As Chapter 3 outlined, static means the system or variable is open through the class definition and not simply through objects. In PHP 4.0, there is no real way to conclude that a variable is static; nonetheless, in PHP 5.0, you can utilize the static modifier.

The :: operator permits you to allude to variables and systems on a class that doesn't yet have any cases or objects made for it. Sample 7.20 shows how you can call a static system using ::, and how the normal technique calling syntax of - > doesn't work, even after an illustration of the class has been made. (PHP doesn't report an error—it simply doesn't work.)

Example 7.20. Utilizing the - >and :: operators to call hypnotize

```
<?php
class Cat {
}
class Hypnotic_Cat extends Cat {
/Constructor
function Hypnotic_Cat( ) {
}
/This function must be called statically
Public static function hypnotize( ) {
echo ("The cat was hypnotized.");
return;
}
}
/Hypnotize all cats
```

```
Hypnotic_Cat::hypnotize( );
$hypnotic_cat = new Hypnotic_Cat( );
/Does nothing
$hypnotic_cat->hypnotize( );
```

It outputs the following:

The feline was hypnotized.

When a strategy is called using the scope resolution operator (::), you can't utilize the $this object to allude to the object in light of the fact that there is no object.

Variable References

In PHP, a variable name focuses to an area in memory that stores the information. There can be more than one variable name indicating the same spot in memory. The ampersand operator (&) is utilized to demonstrate that you're occupied with the area in memory that a variable focuses to rather than its value.

PHP references permit you to make two variables to allude to the same content. In this way, changing the value of one variable can change the value of another. This can make it exceptionally difficult to discover errors in your code, since changing one variable and changes the other.

The same punctuation can be utilized with functions that arrival references. Case 5-21 utilizes this to reference the $some variable.

Example 7.21. Referencing the $some_variable

```
<?php
$some_variable = "Hello World!";
$some_reference = &$some_variable;
$some_reference = "Guten Tag World!";
echo $some_variable;
echo $some_reference;
?>
```

The output is as follows:

```
Guten Tag World!Guten Tag World!
```

Example 7.21 demonstrates that a reference is situated utilizing the & operator and goes before the $ in the current variable. The variable $some_reference then alludes to $some_variable (the memory area where "Hi World!" is placed).

As examined already in this part, variable references are helpful for passing a variable by reference as a parameter to a function. This permits the function to modify the variable in your fundamental code as opposed to modifying a local duplicate/copy that is lost when the function finishes.

Assigning a variable to another variable without using the reference operator results in a copy of the variable being set into another spot in memory. The new variable can be changed without modifying the first variable. While this takes more memory, it's the best approach if you would prefer not to change the first variable's value.

Since you've now comprehensively studied functions and classes, you're prepared to begin working with more perplexing information, for example, arrays. Arrays will be exceptionally valuable when working with information from a database in light of the fact that they can undoubtedly hold the information from an inquiry.

CHAPTER 8

ARRAYS

Variables are awesome for putting away a solitary bit of data, however what happens when you have to store information for an entire arrangement of data, for example, the outcomes of a query? At the point when this happens, uses *arrays*. Arrays are an uncommon sort of variable that stores numerous bits of information. Arrays permit you to get to any of the qualities put away in them individually yet still duplicate and control the array overall. Since they are so valuable, you'll see arrays utilized as often as possible. PHP gives numerous functions to performing basic array assignments, for example, numbering, sorting, and circling through the information.

8.1 Array Fundamentals

To work with arrays, you have to take in two new terms: indexes and elements.

Elements are the qualities that are put away in the array. Every component in the array is referenced by an *index* that differentiates the component from some other one of a kind component in the array. The index value can be a number or a string, but it must be distinctive. You can think about an array like a spreadsheet or a database that has just two sections. The first section interestingly identifies the line in the spreadsheet, while the second segment contains a stored value.

Associative Versus Numeric Indexed Arrays

Numeric arrays uses numbers as their indexes, while acquainted arrays use stings.

At the point when utilizing associative arrays, you must supply an index string every time you include a component. Numeric arrays permit you to simply include the component, and PHP naturally assigns the first free number, beginning at 0. Both types of arrays permit you to include new elements to the array each one in turn.

Associative arrays are pleasant for storing configuration data since their keys can have a significant name.

A typical indication of beginning to get to the estimations of your array at 1 rather than 0 is endeavoring to access the last value and finding it's not there. For example, if you use a numeric array to store five components and let PHP pick the number file values, the last value is put away under the index value of 4.

CHAPTER 9

WORKING WITH MYSQL

It's now your chance to learn how to associate with the MySQL database using the customer tools that accompany MySQL. You might l utilize a web-based element device called phpMyAdmin to modify your database. We'll likewise cover how to utilize SQL to make databases, clients, and tables, and in addition how to modify existing objects in the database.

9.1 MySQL Database

MySQL has its own customer interface, permitting you to move information around and change database design. Note that you ought to utilize a password to sign in. Assigning database clients permits you to constrain access to tables in view of the signed in database client. Each MySQL server can have numerous databases. A web application may utilize its own restrictive database or a standard database like MySQL.

You may have installed MySQL yourself or have entry to it through your ISP. Most ISPs that bolster PHP likewise give a MySQL database to your utilization. Should you have difficulty, check their help pages or contact them to focus association subtle elements establish connection details.

You'll have to know the following:

- The IP location of the database server
- The name of the database
- The username
- The secret key

If you've introduced MySQL on your PC, you'll have the chance to use the defaults from the establishment and the password you chose. This part focuses on two approaches to communicate with MySQL: the order line and phpMyAdmin.

Accessing the Database from the Command Line

One method of communicating with MySQL is through the MySQL command-line customer. Contingent upon which operating system you're using, you have to either open a order shell for Windows (sort cmd from the Run dialog, as indicated in Figure 9.1) on the other hand open a terminal session in Mac OS X and Unix environments.

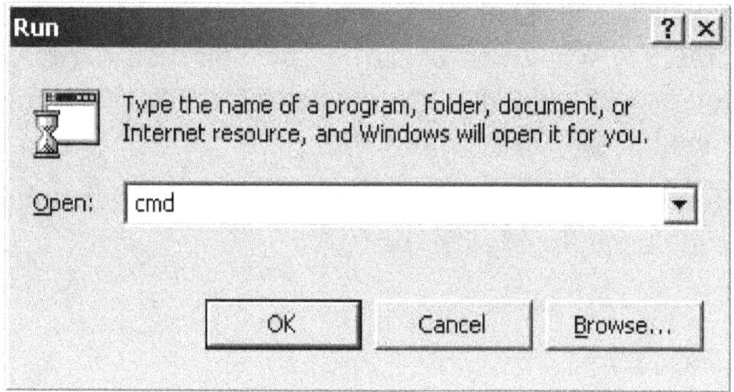
Run
Type the name of a program, folder, document, or Internet resource, and Windows will open it for you.
Open: cmd
OK
Cancel
Browse...

Figure 9.1. Windows Run dialog

When you achieve the command line, type mysql, and press Enter. The syntax for the mysql command is:

mysql - h hostname - u client –p

The default username is root if you've installed MySQL all alone PC. You can overlook the hostname flag and value. Enter your password when MySQL shows the "Enter password" prompt. If the password, username, and hostname are right, you'll see a banner message like that demonstrated in Figure.

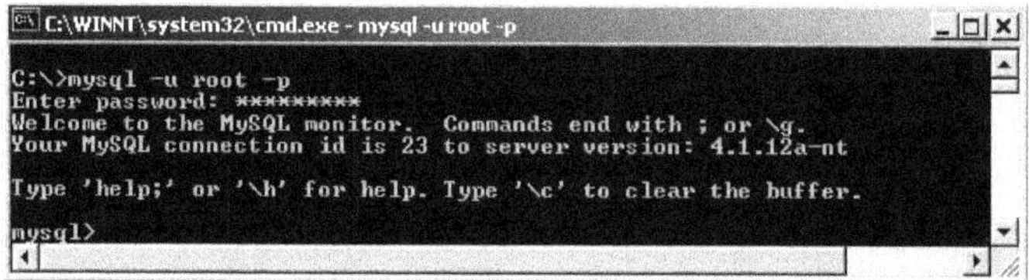
C:\WINNT\system32\cmd.exe - mysql -u root -p
C:\>mysql -u root -p
Enter password: *********
Welcome to the MySQL monitor. Commands end with ; or \g.
Your MySQL connection id is 23 to server version: 4.1.12a-nt
Type 'help;' or '\h' for help. Type '\c' to clear the buffer.
mysql>

The default database that is available after installation is called mysql. The mysql database likewise stores the database client verification information. Try not to erase it! When you began mysql, you didn't specify an association with a specific database. The USE command helps you to do this.

To associate with the mysql database, type the accompanying at the MySQL brief:

```
USE mysql;
```

This returns:

```
Database changed
```

If your ISP supplied a different database name, use that rather than mysql.

9.2 Managing the Database

Now that you're associated with the database, you can make users, databases, and tables. You will not have to make a database or client account if you're using a MySQL server in a hosted environment, and they supplied you with a username and database name.

Creating Users

To make users well beyond the default favored root client, issue the grant command. The grant command runs by this syntax:

GRANT PRIVILEGES ON DATABASE.OBJECTS TO'username'@'hostname' IDENTIFIED BY 'password';

For instance:

GRABALL PRIVILEGES ON *.* TO "michele"@"localhost" IDENTIFIED BY 'secret'; This makes the client michele who can access anything by locally. To change to the michele client, at the mysql command prompt, type:

exit

At that point begin MySQL from the order line with the new username and password. The punctuation for syntax the username and secret word when beginning MySQL is:

mysql - h hostname - u username – p password

Notice that there is no space in the middle of –p and secret word. MySQL can provoke for the secret word if you simply specify the –p banner without a watch-word. If you don't need clients to get to tables other than their own, supplant * in the GRANT ALL PRIVILEGES ON *.* TO "michele" code with the name of the client's database, similar to this:

Concede ALL PRIVILEGES ON store.* TO "michele"@"localhost" IDENTIFIED BY 'mystery'; You'll have to run this line as root or as somebody with authorization. In this code, the word store associates to the database name where benefits are allocated, which you'll make in the following area.

Creating a MySQL Database

You're going to make a database called store. The CREATE DATABASE command functions like this:

Create DATABASE store;

If this works, you'll get an outcome like this one:

Query OK, 1 row influenced (0.03 sec)

Database names can't contain any spaces. On Unix servers such as Linux and Mac OS X, database names are case-sensitive as well.

To begin using this database, type:

Use store;

You will get the outcome:

Database changed.

Believing you've done everything accurately, you'll be set up with new information, and it will be chosen for use. Making tables to store information is an imperative idea, so that is the place we're heading!

9.3 Using phpMyAdmin

The tool phpMyAdmin, accessible from http://www.phpmyadmin.net/, permits you to control a MySQL database through your web program. All that is needed is a web server with PHP installed and a MySQL database to control it.

To introduce phpMyAdmin, take after these strides:

1. Click Downloads from the primary page.

2. Download the archive document, for example, all-languages.tar.gz (Unix archived) or alllanguages. zip (Windows ZIP design).

3. Unpack the archive (counting subdirectories) to a directory on your PC.

4. Send them to your ISP account where PHP records can be executed. Alternately, if you have a web server installed locally, relocate them to a catalog in the document root with a consistent name, for example, *myadmin*.

5. To build up phpMyAdmin, make a directory called config inside of the myadmin directory. On Linux frameworks, execute these commands rather to make the directory, and set the systems to permit the setup program to modify the confuguration document:

compact disc myadmin

mkdir config

chmod o+rw config

cp config.inc.php config/

chmod o+w config/config.inc.php

6. In your web program, explore to http://localhost/myadmin/scripts/setup.php.

You'll see a screen like the one displayed in the Figure.

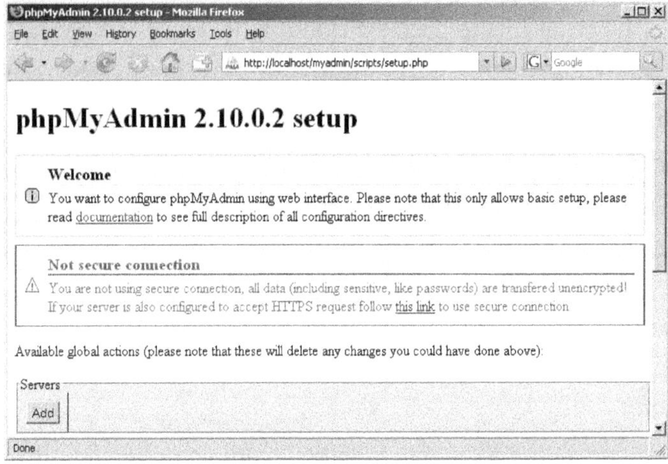

Figure 9.3. The phpMyAdmin setup creates the configuration file for phpMyAdmin

7. In the Servers segment, tap the Add button. The Server setup page shows as demonstrated in Figure 9.4.

8. A large portion of the default values can be left alone. You do need to enter the passsword for the root MySQL client in the "password for config auth" field.

9. Select "cookie" from Authentication sort to limit access to your MySQL information to just clients with a MySQL account.

10. Click "Add."

11. Click “Save” from the Configuration section to save your progressions to the configuration file.

12. Duplicate the config.inc.php file to myadmin.

13. Remove the config directory.

14. In your web program, explore to http://localhost/myadmin/index.php. Your web program shows a login page like the one demonstrated in Figure.

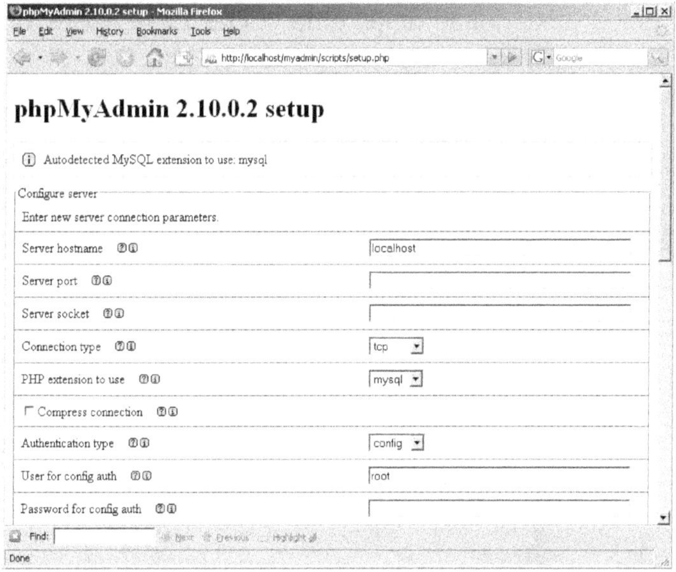

Figure 9.4. Defining the connection details for your MySQL server

When introduced and associated with the database, phpMyAdmin’s primary page seems to be same to the one displayed in Figure 9.6.

You can choose any configured databases from the drop-down list marked Databases.

The administrator gives a simple approach to perceive how your database is arranged and what objects exist, (for example, tables), and you're even offered the choice to include tables through the graphical interface. Through the PHP administrator, you can make new databases and tables, run queries, and showcase server statistics.

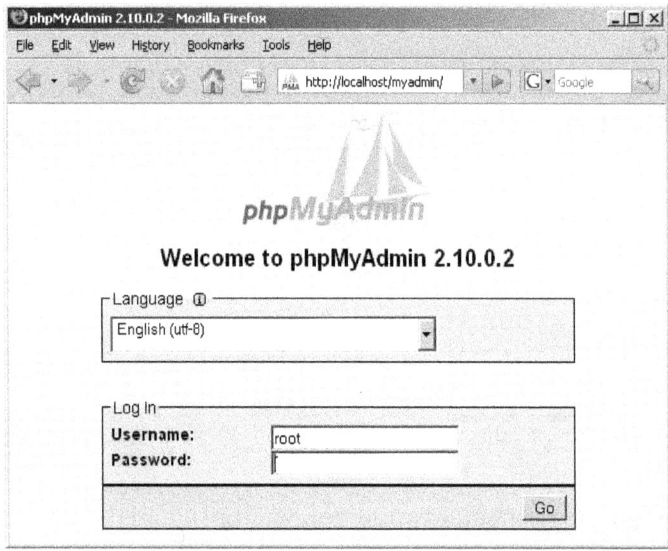

Figure 9.5. The login page restricts access to your database

The figure demonstrates the tables in the test database we'll be making in this section. If your database makes use of a different name, substitute that name for "test." Click on the creators table on the left to get more details on that table.

Tapping on the creators table shows its table structure. This screen gives an simple approach to imagine the design of a database, especially if it's a database that you didn't make yourself.

To see the content of a table, tap on the Browse tab. Figure 9.8 demonstrates the browse tab for the creators table.

The web admin tool gives an interface that is simple to use either for going through your database and making new objects or for modifying data. You may find the graphical interface to be an invigorating change from the content based command line of the mysql client.

We're presently going to acquaint you with essential database structure so you have some basic yet vital knowledge of databases. We'll give you a strong comprehension of the language that is utilized to communicate with the database, SQL. The initial phase in setting up your database is to make some database tables. At that point you'll figure out how to include, view, and change information.

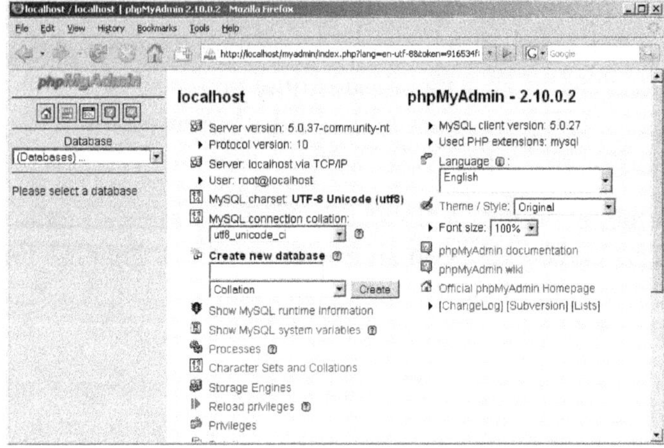

Figure 9.6. Selecting a database to administer in php-MyAdmin

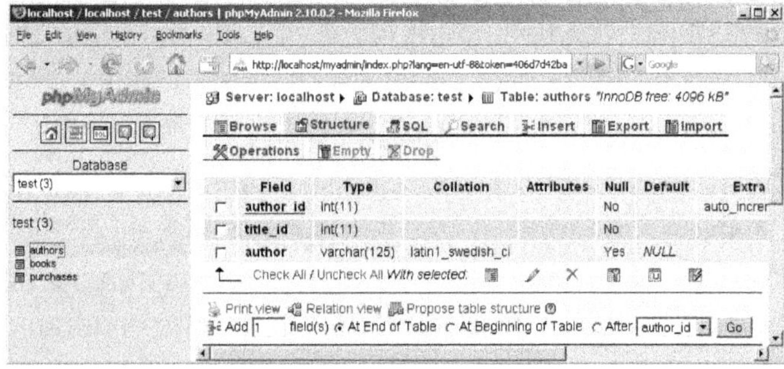

Figure 9.7. The objects in the test database and the authors table structure

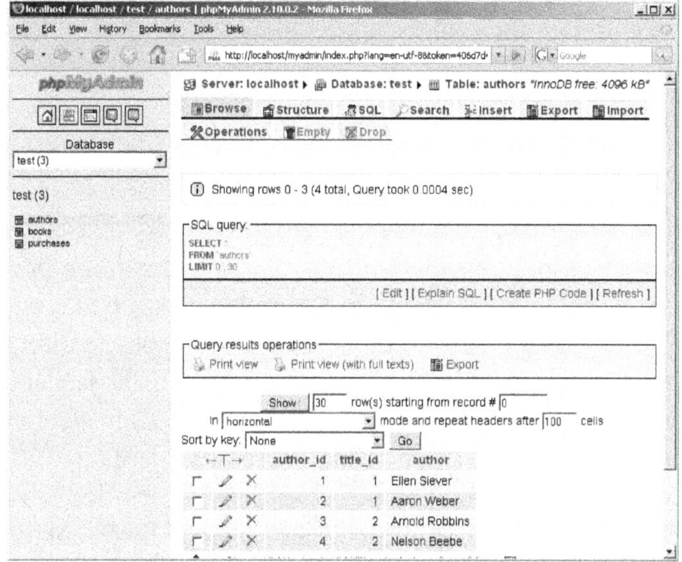

The data in the authors table and the query used to generate it

9.4 Database Concepts

Databases are a vault for data. They stand out at overseeing and controlling organized data. *Structured information* is an approach to arrange related pieces of data, which we examined already in Chapters 3–6. The fundamental types of structured data, which can as well be called *data structures*, include:

- Files
- Lists

- Arrays
- Records
- Trees
- Tables

Each of these fundamental structures has numerous varieties and considers different operations to be performed on the information. A simple approach to comprehend this idea is to think about the telephone directory (phone book). It's the most common database, and it contains a few items of data—name, address, and telephone number, and in addition every telephone subscriber in a specific range. Telephone directories have advanced, and a few individuals might have bolded names, however generally, every entry in the telephone directory takes the same structure.

If you think about the physical printed version telephone directory in comparable terms as a database, the telephone directory is a table, which contains a record for every subscriber. Every subscriber's record contains three fields (otherwise called attributes or columns): name, address as well as telephone number. These records are identified by the name field, which is called the key field. The telephone directory is arranged by alphabets through last names first; check Figure 9.9 for how a distinctive record and distinctive fields show in your database based on telephone directory's analogy. While the information in a MySQL database isn't kept in any specific order, it can be queried in order.

Name	Address	Phone Number
Davis, Michele	7505 N. Linksway FxPnt 53217	414-352-4818
Meyer, Simon	5802 Beard Avenue S 55419	612-925-6897
Phillips, Jon	4204 Zenith Avenue S 55416	612-924-8020
Phillips, Peter	6200 Bayard Avenue HgldPk 55411	651-668-2251

Figure 9.9. Phone book record and fields

If you took the same information from the phone book and place it into a database, you could assemble questions e.g. who has the telephone number 651-668-2251, or everybody in a specific postal division or zip code who has the last name Davis. This kind of database is similar to a major spreadsheet; it can be known as a flat-file database, which implies every database is self-contained in one table. Since the 1970s, relational databases for handling information have replaced flat files. They sustain various tables, connected together as required.

9.5 Structured Query Language

Since you've characterized a table, you can add information to it. MySQL will keep track of all details. To manage information, use the Structured Query Language (SQL) commands.

Since it's been intended to effortlessly portray the relationship between rows and tables, the database uses SQL to modify information in the tables.

SQL is a standard language used with most databases

e.g. MySQL, Oracle, or Microsoft SQL Server. It was created specifically as a language used to recover, include, and manage information that stays in databases. We'll get into the details of MySQL in the next chapter, but we'll start with some simple commands that are easy to use. We're going to commence with making tables.

Making Tables

Make use of the table commands to specify the structure of new database tables.

When you make a database table, every segment has a couple of choices as well as data types and column names. Values that must be supplied when adding information to a table are specified through the NOT NULL keyword. The PRIMARY KEY keyword tells MySQL which segment to use as a key field. Subsequently, you have MySQL assign key values using the AUTO_INCREMENT keyword automatically.

To make these tables, type and paste the code into the MySQL command line client. Later chapters contain essential data if you're occupied with running the SQL code in the accompanying examples. It clarifies how to access the MySQL client, allot security permissions through the GRANT charge, make a database, and select it for use.

Example 9.1. Making the books and authorss tables

```
Create TABLE books (
title_id INT NOT NULL AUTO_INCREMENT,
title VARCHAR (150),
pages INT,
PRIMARY KEY (title_id));

MAKE TABLE authors (
author_id INT NOT NULL AUTO_INCREMENT,
title_id INT NOT NULL,
author VARCHAR (125),
PRIMARY KEY (author_id));
```

If all is well, you'll see output that requires MySQL to make a table called "books," and it'll look like Example 9.2 (the time the inquiry takes to run may be different than 0.06 sec):

Example 9.2. Making Sample Data

```
mysql> CREATE TABLE books (
- > title_id INT NOT NULL AUTO_INCREMENT,
- > title VARCHAR (150),
- > pages INT,
- > PRIMARY KEY (title_id));
```

Query OK, 0 rows affected (0.06 sec)

The code to make the books table separates as takes after:

• The first section, called title_id, is a number/integer. The auto_increment keyword is a special value assigned to this field automatically during line insertion.

• The title column holds content up to 150 characters.

• The pages column is a whole number.

• The PRIMARY KEY trait tells MySQL which field is the key value.

The essential key must be one of a kind and not NULL. All tables ought to have a primaryl key, as it permits MySQL to accelerate access when you recover information from multiple tables then again a specific column utilizing the key quality. MySQL does this by utilizing an extraordinary information structure called a *index*. An *index* works like an easy route for finding a record, similar to a card catalog in a library. To verify your table columns, use DESCRIBE:

Depict books;

Adding Data to a Table

The INSERT command is used to include information. Its syntax is *INSERT INTO table COLUMNS ([columns]) VALUES ([values]);*. This syntax shows which table information should be added to, the columns, and a list of the values. If the segments aren't specified, the values must be in the same request in which they were defined when the table was made (provided that you don't skip any section values). There are specific principles for how you handle information to populate your database using SQL commands:

- Numeric values shouldn't be cited.
- String values ought to dependably be cited.
- Date and time values ought to dependably be cited.
- Functions shouldn't be cited.
- NULL ought to never be cited.

Finally, if a column isn't given a value, it's thus viewed as NULL unless a default exists for the section. If a section can't have NULL (it was made with NOT Invalid) and you don't specify a value, an error happens.

E.g.:

INSERT INTO books VALUES (1,"Linux in a Nutshell",112);

INSERT INTO authors VALUES (NULL,1,"Ellen Siever");

INSERT INTO authors VALUES (NULL,1,"Aaron Weber");

Provided that there were no errors, you ought to get:

mysql> INSERT INTO books VALUES (1,"Linux in a

Nutshell",112);

Query OK, 1 row affected (0.00 sec)

mysql> INSERT INTO authors VALUES (NULL,1,"Ellen Siever");

Query OK, 1 row affected (0.00 sec)

mysql> INSERT INTO creators VALUES (NULL,1,"Aaron Weber");

Query OK, 1 line influenced (0.00 sec)

At the point when including information, you must specify every one of the columns regardless of the possibility that you aren't supplying a value for everyone. Despite the fact that we didn't supply the author_id field and we let MySQL assign it for us, regardless we needed to leave a placeholder for it.

Similarly, we include the other book:

INSERT INTO books VALUES (2,"Classic Shell Scripting",256);

INSERT INTO authors VALUES (NULL,2,"Arnold Robbins");

INSERT INTO authors VALUES (NULL,2,"Nelson Beebe");

This gives us two rows in the books table. Since you know how to make a table as well as enter information into it, you'll have to know how to view that data.

Table Definition Manipulation

Once you've made a table and began storing data in it, you may find that you have to implement an improvement to the column types. For instance, you may find that a field you thought would require just 30 characters really needs 100. You could begin all over and reclassify the table, however you'd lose all your information. Thankfully, MySQL permits you to modify column types without losing your information. The following examples presume that you've made the database tables in this section.

Renaming a table

To rename a table, *use ALTER table RENAME new table*. In this illustration, we are renaming the table from books to productions:

Modify TABLE books RENAME productions;

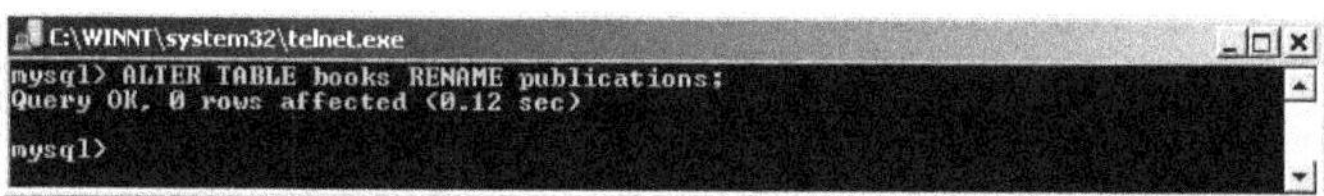

Renaming a table

Querying the Database

Having information in tables doesn't benefit much if you can't view what's in them. The SELECT command specifies which table(s) to query and which row(s) to view based on specific conditions. The sentence structure of SELECT will be SELECT *columns FROM ta-*

bles [WHERE CLAUSE];[ORDER BY CLAUSE];.

Sections show a rundown of segments to show from the chosen/selected tables. The WHERE proviso alternatively confines which lines are chosen. *WHERE* gives cutoff points to the results that are returned from a query. For instance, rows can be dismissed if a field doesn't break even with an exacting value or is not exactly or more noteworthy than a quality. The ORDER BY proviso permits you to sort the returned data in coveted ways. Fields from numerous tables can be compelled to be equivalent. If various tables are incorporated in a SELECT statement without a WHERE clause, the subsequent set turns into the Cartesian item, in which each row in the first table is returned with all columns in the second table, followed by the same thing for the second row in the first table. To put it another way, that is a great deal of results!

Modifying Database Data

If you commit an error, say, by entering the wrong number of pages for a book, you can change the information by utilizing the UPDATE commands. There are many different motivations to upgrade a table, for example, a client changing his password.

UPDATE uses the same WHERE clause as the SELECT statement, however it includes a SET commands that specifies segment value.

Erasing Database Data

The DELETE command is utilized to erase columns or records in a table. It takes the same WHERE clause as UPDATE however erases any columns that match. Without the WHERE clause, you'd have an "uh oh!" minute on the grounds that every one of the records in the table would be erased.

CHAPTER 10

DATABASE BEST PRACTICES

Since you have MySQL up and running and have made a database, we should talk about database design and protecting your databases. As you most likely are aware, it is imperative to have your data backed up. Adding MySQL to PHP and combining the applications for your dynamic website is an incredible beginning. However, it helps massively to structure your database accurately. If you have security, information integrity, and backups, you have the most significant bits of a database. We'll examine security in later chapters.

10.1 Database Design

Designing your database rightfully is imperative to your application's exceptional performance. Just as putting the printer the distance over your office is ineffective, setting information in poor connections makes work less productive in light of the fact that your database server will waste time searching for information. At the point when thinking about your database, consider the types of inquiries will be asked when your database is used. For example, what are the details around an item available to be purchased? Alternately, is this a legitimate username and password?

Relational Databases

MySQL is a relational database. A vital element of relational frameworks is that information can be spread over a few tables, instead of our level document telephone directory sample. Related information is put away in isolated tables and permits you to put them together by utilizing a key regular to both tables. The key is the connection between the tables. The selection of a primary key is a standout amongst the most basic choices you'll make in designing another database.

The most imperative idea that you have to comprehend is that you must guarantee that the chose key is exceptional. If it's conceivable that two records (past, present, or future) have the same quality for a property, don't utilize that characteristic as an essential key. Counting key fields from another table to form a connection between tables is known as a remote key relationship, similar to a supervisor to workers or a client to a buy.

Since you have separate tables that store related information, you have to consider the quantity of things in every table that identifies with things in different tables.

Relationship Types

Databases connections are quantified with the accompanying classifications:

- One-to-one connections
- One-to-numerous connections
- Many-to-numerous connections

We'll talk about each of these connections and give a sample. If you think about a family structure when considering connections, you're on top of things. At the point when you invest energy alone with one parent, that is a specific kind of relationship; when you invest energy with both your parents, that is another. If you get a significant accomplice and every one of you—your parents, you, and your accomplice—do something together, that is another relationship. This is indistinguishable to the basin similarity. All those different sorts of connections are similar to specific cans that hold the flow of your connections. In the database world, this is the information you've made.

One-on-one relationships

In a one-on-one relationship, each item is identified with one and one and only other thing. Within the instance of an online book shop, a coordinated relationship exists between clients and their delivery addresses. Every client must have precisely one shipping address.

Standardization

Contemplating about how your information is connected and the most effective approach to arrange it is called standardization. Standardization of information is breaking it separated in light of the coherent connections to minimize the duplication of information. For the most part, copied information squanders space and makes upkeep an issue. Should you change data that is copied, there's the chance that you miss a part and danger irregularities in your database. It's conceivable to have a lot of something to be thankful for, however; databases setting every piece of information in their own tables would take an excessive amount of handling time, and questions would be convoluted. Discovering equalization in the middle of is the objective. While the telephone directory illustration is extremely basic, the sort of information that you prepare with a site page can advantage incredibly from intelligently gathering related information. We should proceed with the online book shop sample. The site needs to stay informed concerning the client's information, including login, address, and telephone number, and in addition data about the books, including the title, writer, number of pages, and when every title was obtained. Begin by putting the greater part of this data in one table. While joining the information into one table may appear like a smart thought, it squanders space in the database and makes overhauling the information repetitive. All the client information is rehashed for every buy. A book is constrained to just two writers. In this case, we're utilizing books that have two writers rather than only one. Also, if the client moves, his location changes, and each of his entrances in the table must be redesigned.

Types of Normalization

To standardize a database, begin with the most essential guidelines of standardization and move forward regulated. The progressions of standardization are in three stages, called structures.

The primary step, called First Normal Form (1NF or FNF), must be done before the second typical structure. In like manner, the third ordinary structure can't be finished before the second. The standardization procedure includes getting your information into similarity with the three dynamic typical structures.

- ✓ First Normal Form

For your database to be in First Normal Form, it must fulfill three necessities. No table may have rehashing sections that contain the same sort of information, and all segments must contain stand out worth. There must be an essential key that exceptionally characterizes columns. It can be one section or a few segments, contingent upon what number of segments are expected to extraordinarily identify columns.

- ✓ Second Normal Form

While the first ordinary structure manages repetition of information over a flat column, the Second Normal Form (or 2NF) arrangements with repetition of information in vertical segments.

Ordinary structures are dynamic. To accomplish Second Normal Form, your tables must as of now be in First Normal Form. For a database table to be in Second Normal Structure, you must identify any segments that rehash their qualities over numerous columns. Those segments should be set in their own table and referenced by a key esteem in the first table. Another state of mind of this is if there are properties in the table that aren't subject to the essential key.

✓ Third Normal Form

If you've taken after the First and Second Normal Form process, you should not have to do anything with your database to fulfill the Third Normal Form (or 3NF) principles. In Third Normal Form, you're searching for information in your tables that is not completely subordinate on the essential key, yet reliant on another esteem in the table. Where this applies to your tables isn't instantly clear. In Table 8-8, the parts of the locations can be considered as not being straightforwardly identified with the client. The road address depends on the postal division, the postal division on the city, lastly, the city on the state. The Third Normal Form obliges that each of these be split out into isolated tables.

As you may have seen, the Third Normal Form uproots much more information repetition, be that as it may, at the expense of effortlessness and execution. In this illustration, do you truly expect the city and road names to change frequently? In this circumstance, the Third Ordinary Form still forestalls incorrect spelling of city and road names. Since it's your database, you settle on the level of harmony in the middle of standardization and the pace or effortlessness of your database.

Since we've secured the important points of how your information is laid out, we can dive into the subtle elements of how segments are characterized.

Column Data Types

Despite the fact that databases store the same data that you gather and process in PHP, databases need fields to be set to specific sorts of information when they're made.

Keep in mind, PHP isn't strongly typed, however most databases are!

10.2 Backing Up and Restoring Data

A data type is the classification of a specific kind of data. When you read, you're used to traditions, for example, images, letters, and numbers. Thusly, it's simple to recognize different sorts of information in light of the fact that you utilize images along with numbers and letters. You can tell initially whether a number is a rate, a period, or a measure of cash. The images that help you to comprehend a rate, time, or measure of cash are that information's sort. A database uses inside codes to stay informed regarding the different sorts of information it forms.

Numerous programming languages require the software designer to announce the data type of each information object, and most database frameworks require the client to specify the sort of every information field. The accessible information sorts fluctuate from one programming dialect to another, and from one database application to another. Be that as it may, the three fundamental sorts of information—numbers, dates/times, and strings—exist in some structure.

The numeric ID fields, consolidated with a wellspring of extraordinary numbers, give a method for ensuring that the key field is special. Specifying the auto_increment decisive word at the point when making a section is an incredible approach to produce an one of a kind ID for a segment. For case, if there are two creators with the name John Smith, and you utilize their names as a key, you'd have an issue staying informed regarding which John Smith you're utilizing. Keeping keys one of a kind is a critical piece of verifying you have the right information in your database.

Backing up and Restoring Data

Indeed, even the best-kept up databases once in a while gets problems. Tool failures, specifically, can truly destroy into your site pages. Since you're using a database, simply moving down the documents (HTML, PHP, and pictures) on your web server isn't sufficient. There's nothing more terrible than advising your web clients that they need to return data, for example, their records, or needing to reproduce your list things. Having a complete reinforcement can have the effect between 60 minutes of downtime and needing to rehash.

Duplicating Database Files

You can likewise do a straightforward document reinforcement of your MySQL database's data files, in the same way that you can go down your HTML and PHP documents. If you can go down documents, you can move down the MySQL database documents.

We don't prescribe this strategy for moving a database starting with one machine then onto the next server, since different variants of MySQL may anticipate that these documents will be in a different design. MySQL stores its data files in an exceptional information registry that is normally situated in C:\Program Files\MySQL\MySQL Server 4.1\data\[database_name] on Windows and in/var/lib/mysql on Unix variations, for example, Linux and Mac OS X. Close down the MySQL benefit before doing a record duplicate reinforcement to ensure that all documents are from the same point in time while doing your reinforcement.

To completely move down and restore a MySQL database utilizing your current data files, all the documents must be supplanted in the same registry from which they were went down. At that point the database must be restarted.

The mysqldump Command

It's ideal to utilize the MySQL command line for making complete database reinforcements. The same instruments you'll use to go down and restore can likewise be utilized to change stages or move your database starting with one server then onto the next; mysqldump makes a content document containing the SQL statements needed to remake the database objects and supplement the information. The mysqldump charge is open from the summon line and takes parameters for going down a solitary table, a solitary database, or everything. The order's sentence structure is:

mysqldump - u client - p objects_to_backup

The mysqldump command creates the reinforcement output to standard out (which by default just prints to the screen). Specify a client who has admittance to the object you need to go down. You will be incited for the related watchword for that client.

Divert this output to a document utilizing the more prominent than (>) character took after by a filename.

Backing up

We're going to demonstrate to you the charges to go down a database called store from the shell brief.

mysqldump - u root - p store > my_backup_of_store.sql

This tells mysqldump to sign into the database as the

root client and to go down the store database. You will be incited for the root watchword that you chose amid establishment. The output of the command is put in a record called my_backup_of_store. sql with the assistance of the sidetrack character, otherwise called the more prominent than image (>).

Restoring a MySQL backup

The uplifting news is that it's not difficult to reproduce your database from a mysqldump record. The substances of the backup record are essentially SQL statements what's more, can thusly be prepared by the MySQL charge line customer to restore the moved down information.

If you did a reinforcement of your database utilizing mysqldump - all-databases to a record called

my_backup.sql, you could restore your database:

mysql - u root - p < my_backup.sql

If you did a particular reinforcement of one and only database, it's some more intricate. To restore that kind of reinforcement record, utilize the - D charge line switch:

mysql - u root - p - D store < my_backup.sql

Since you know how to restore default dump records, we can proceed onward to some different applications with respect to sending out and importing information.

Working with other formats

Albeit working with SQL-based records is advantageous, there may be times when you need to spare your information in different configurations. Case in point, a typical strategy for speaking to a rundown of information is in CSV (comma-isolated qualities) position. The mysqldump summon underpins this configuration. You should do nothing more than specify the *- no-create info, - tab, furthermore, - fields-terminated by arguments*:

mysqldump - u root - p - no-make data - tab=/home/ jon - fields-ended by=', 'store

This tellss mysqldump to produce separate documents for every table in the store database.

They'll all be put in the catalog/home/jon. Every document's name will be the name of the table that is being sent out. Every document contains the records in the separate table isolated by the comma character (,) that was specified on the order line.

The mysqlimport command

When you're setting up your database, you may need to acquire information from another database or a spreadsheet in CSV position. For instance, if you're putting forth books for deal, you may get the current index of books. Case 8-2 demonstrates the book titles in CSV design.

To import the information showed in Example 8-2, utilization the mysqlimport summon:

mysqlimport - u root - p - fields-ended by=',' store books.txt

The fundamental bit of the filename (excluding the way or document augmentation) decides the name of the table. In the past sample, the table name is books. The table must as of now exist, or a lapse shows. Another valuable essential word is ENCLOSED BY roast;, which permits you to specify characters, for example, twofold quotes (") that encase every field in the record. This is valuable for staying away from the problem with a book title like Exemplary Shell Scripting, Second Edition, which would somehow bring about mysqlimport to process the Second Edition segment of the title as the begin of the following field.

Best backup practices

Contingent upon how basic your information is and how regularly it transforms, you can focus how regularly to back it up. Generally speaking, week by week, bi-week by week, and month to month are the most widely recognized plans. If your business is totally reliant on your database, you ought to do a week after week, if not day by day, reinforcement plan. Additionally, keeping a duplicate of the information in a different area is a smart thought in the occasion of huge scale catastrophes, for example, a flame. A customer of our own keeps bi-month to month reinforcements in a flame resistant safe at the workplace, though another customer sends the information to a reinforcement administration. A reinforcement administration can utilize physical hard drives, tapes, or CDs, or can sign into your server and perform the reinforcement electronically.

10.3 Advanced SQL

In this segment, we'll present database ideas that, while not entirely fundamental for building up your sites, can enhance execution and make your inquiries more adaptable.

Indexes

Records work the same way that a file of a book meets expectations. If you were to search for the magic word "Make TABLE" without a file, you'd have to invest a great deal of energy looking over the pages of the book searching for an area that may be relevant. Then you'd need to check the whole segment. This absolutely isn't an effective utilization of your time or the database engine's. The arrangement is a list.

The information in a list is sorted and composed to make discovering a specific esteem as brisk as would be prudent. Since the qualities are sorted, if you're searching for something specific, the database can quit looking when it discovers a quality bigger than the item for which you're looking.

You confront the same issues as a book does, however. If a record is so extraordinary, why not record everything? There are various reasons:

• There's just a limited amount of space accessible.

• When composing books, it gets to be ineffective to produce and keep up an enormous, widely inclusive index.

• Too much information in the file implies it takes more time to peruse the file when selecting information.

In this way, some insightful choices about which fields to file in your tables must be made. Every file obliges its own particular data file for capacity, which can include a touch of preparing time when the substance of an ordered field changes in the database.

When indexed are used

If you do a basic SELECT statement without a WHERE provision, a file won't be utilized.

There are three noteworthy zones where a list can be used:

In a WHERE clause

For instance, the inquiry SELECT * FROM creators WHERE creator = 'Ellen Siever'; would utilize a record on the creator section if it's accessible.

In an ORDER BY clause

For instance, the inquiry SELECT * FROM contacts ORDER BY creator; would utilize an record on the creator segment if it's accessible.

In MIN and MAX clause

For instance, the question would utilize a list if the segment that is specified in the MIN or MAX function has a record.

Simply remember, files must be defined before they can be used.

Where to specify the index

Database records can be specified as a component of the CREATE TABLE command, or they can be added to a current table by utilizing extraordinary SQL summons. If the list is made as a major aspect of the CREATE TABLE summon, it's specified toward the end of the code piece:

UNIQUE authind (creator)

The UNIQUE command makes a list on the creator name field. Then again, not all lists are one of a kind.

Multicolumn indexes

It's additionally feasible to make MySQL lists that use more than one section. A multicolumn one of a kind list guarantees that the mix of section qualities is remarkable.

The best sections to list are those that are prone to be

utilized as a part of the WHERE statement, particularly if you realize that certain mixes of keys will be utilized. Those are great sections to add to a multicolumn list. Request the sections in a multicolumn record with the goal that sections utilized every now and again start things out. MySQL utilizes a multicolumn file to accelerate an inquiry regardless of the fact that just the first estimation of the list is utilized.

Essential files are additionally novel. Stand out essential file is permitted per table. Be that as it may, you can have the same number of special files as your heart wants.

We're going to do an inquiry with a specific WHERE condition, and afterward utilize EXPLAIN to get insights about how it was prepared by MySQL:

SELECT * FROM creators WHERE creator = 'Arnold Robbins';

The EXPLAIN output gives an abundance of data about how MySQL prepared the question.

It tells you:

• That you're utilizing the creators table.

• The question sort is ALL, so every record is filtered to check for the right esteem.

• The possible_keys is NULL in light of the fact that no record matches.

- The key utilized by this question is as of now NULL.
- The key_len is the key length; as of now NULL, as no key was utilized.
- The ref section shows which segments or constants are utilized with the key; at present NULL.
- The quantity of columns that must be looked through.

Notice that a large number of the qualities have changed with respect to the indexing:

- ref implies that lines with coordinating list qualities are read from this table for matches.
- possible_keys shows a conceivable key of authind.
- key shows that the authind key was utilized.
- key_len shows the length of the key as 126.
- ref lets you know that a consistent key is being utilized.
- columns demonstrate that one line was sought, which is a great deal not exactly some time recently.

The correlation demonstrates that adding the index spares a great deal of processing time even for little tables.

Selecting with the LEFT JOIN ON Clause

We've talked about performing joins in our SELECT statements utilizing the WHERE provision, be that as it may, there's another approach to join tables. Rather than utilizing the WHERE pivotal word, LEFT JOIN ON can be utilized to perform left or external join. A left join essentially permits you to inquiry two tables that are connected together by a relationship, yet permits one of the tables to return lines regardless of the possibility that there isn't a coordinating line in the other table. Utilizing the book shop tables as an illustration, you may need to make an inquiry that profits clients and their buys, additionally records clients who have yet to buy anything.

Using the punctuation:

SELECT fields FROM left_table LEFT JOIN right_table ON left_table.field_id = right_

table.field_id; your objective could be refined like this:

SELECT * FROM clients LEFT JOIN buys ON users.user_id =

purchases.user_id;

If you'd like to attempt this inquiry, you'll have to make the clients table and include some information:

Make TABLE clients (

user_id int(11) NOT NULL auto_increment,

first_name varchar(100) default NULL,

last_name varchar(100) default NULL,

username varchar(45) default NULL,

secret key varchar(32) default NULL,

Essential KEY (user_id)

);

Embed INTO clients VALUES

(1,'Michele','Davis','mdavis',NULL),(2,'Jon','Phillips','jphillips',NULL);

While doing an ordinary database query that connections two tables, if both tables don't incorporate the key qualities for the field being joined, nothing is returned for the passage.

Using Database Functions

Much the same as there are functions in PHP; you can likewise utilize functions inside of your MySQL questions. We'll talk about a few classifications of functions, beginning with string functions.

The other real classifications you'll find out about are date and time modification functions.

String functions

Since you'll as often as possible work with strings, MySQL gives numerous functions to doing a mixed bag of undertakings. You'll for the most part utilize the string functions with information that is being returned from question. Nonetheless, it's conceivable to utilize them without notwithstanding referencing a table.

Concatenation. Much the same as the procedure of assembling strings with the PHP spot operator

(.), which is a period, MySQL can glue together strings fromdata fields with the CONCAT function.

Case in point, if you need to give back a solitary field that joins the title with the number of pages, you could utilize CONCAT.

Exchanges

Exchanges compel different changes to a database to be dealt with as a solitary unit of work. Either the greater parts of the progressions are acknowledged or they are all discarded. No other session can get to a table while you have an exchange transparent rolled out improvements to that table. In your session, you quickly see any progressions made to the information if you select the same information after an upgrade.

If you're utilizing an exchange fit stockpiling motor, for example, InnoDB or BDB, you may utilize the begin exchange summon to start an exchange. The exchange is finished when you either confer or rollback your progressions. Two orders control finishing your exchange. The confer order spares the progressions to the database. The rollback order forsakes the progressions.

Case 8-19 makes an exchange skilled table, embeds information, begins an exchange, erases information, and moves back an exchange.

Since the exchange was moved back, you can even now select the information:

SELECT * FROM books_innodb WHERE (title_id = 1 OR title_id = 2);

This profits the accompanying:

+ - + - - + - +

| title_id | title | pages |

+ - + - - + - +

| 1 | Linux in a Nutshell | 476 |

| 2 | Classic Shell Scripting | 558 |

+ - + - - + - +

2 columns in set (0.05 sec)

Sample 8-19. Utilizing an exchange

Make TABLE `books_innodb` (

`title_id` int(11) NOT NULL auto_increment,

`title` varchar(150) default NULL,

`pages` int(11) default NULL,

Essential KEY (`title_id`)

) ENGINE=InnoDB DEFAULT CHARSET=latin1;

Embed INTO `books_innodb` (`title_id`, `title`, `pages`) VALUES

(1, ‘Linux in a Nutshell’, 476),

(2, ‘Exemplary Shell Scripting’, 558);

begin exchange;

erase from books_innodb where title_id = 1;

erase from books_innodb where title_id = 2;.

CHAPTER 11

GETTING PHP TO TALK TO MYSQL

Now that you're open to utilizing the MySQL customer devices to control information in the database, you can start utilizing PHP to show and modify information from the database.

PHP has standard functions for working with the database.

In the first place, we're going to talk about PHP's inherent database functions. We'll likewise demonstrate to you the most effective method to utilize The PHP Extension and Application Repository (PEAR) database functions that give the capacity to utilize the same functions to get to any bolstered database. This kind of adaptability originates from a procedure called deliberation. In programming interfaces, reflection simplifies an intricate connection. It lives up to expectations by uprooting any unimportant parts of the collaboration, permitting you to focus on the essential parts. PEAR's DB classes are one such database interface reflection.

11.1 The process

The data you have to sign into a database is decreased to the absolute minimum.

This standard arrangement permits you to cooperate with MySQL, and in addition different databases utilizing the same functions. So also, other MySQL-specific functions are supplanted with non specific ones that know how to converse with numerous databases. Case in point, the

MySQL-specific interface function is:

mysql_connect($db_host, $db_username, $db_password);

versus PEAR's DB interface function:

$connection = DB::connect("mysql://$db_username:$db_password@$db_host/$db_database");

The same essential data is available in both charges, yet the PEAR function additionally specifies the sort of databases to which to join. You can join with MySQL on the other hand other upheld databases. We'll examine both association techniques in point of interest.

In this section, you'll figure out how to unite with a MySQL server fromPHP, how to utilize PHP to get to and recover put away information, and how to accurately show data to the client.

The Process

The essential strides of performing an inquiry, whether utilizing the mysql order line apparatus or

PHP, are the same:

- Connect to the database.
- Select the database to utilize.
- Build a SELECT statement.
- Perform the question.
- Display the outcomes.

We'll stroll through each of these progressions for both plain PHP and PEAR functions.

Assets

At the point when associating with a MySQL database, you will utilize two new assets. The principal is the connection identifier that holds the greater part of the data important to associate with the database for a dynamic association. The other asset is the outcomes asset. It contains all data needed to recover results from a dynamic database question's outcome set.

You'll be making and allocating both assets in this part.

Querying the Database with PHP Functions

In this area, we acquaint how with associate with a MySQL database with PHP. It's truly basic, and we'll start instantly with illustrations, however we ought to speak quickly about what really happens. When you have a go at joining with a MySQL database, the MySQL server validates you in view of your username and secret word. PHP handles uniting to the database for you, and it permits you to begin performing questions and gathering information quickly.

As in Chapter 8, we'll require the same bits of data to associate with the database:

- The IP location of the database server
- The name of the database
- The username
- The secret word

Before proceeding onward, verify you can sign into your database utilizing the MySQL charge line customer.

Figure 9-1 shows how the progressions of the database collaboration identify with the two sorts of assets. Building the SELECT statement happens before the third function call, yet it is not indicated. It's finished with plain PHP code, not a MySQL-specific PHP function.

11.2 Querying the Database with PHP Functions

The principal thing you have to do is associate with the database and check to verify there's an association.

Counting the document that you set up to store your association data permits you to utilize the variables rather than hardcoded qualities when you call the

mysql_connect function, as indicated in Example 9-4. We're amassing one document, db_ test.php, by including these code pieces.

The mysql_connect function takes the database have, username, and secret word as parameters. If the association is effective, a connection to a database is returned. FALSE is returned if an association can't be made. Check the arrival quality from the function to verify there's an association. If there's an issue, for example, an inaccurate secret key, print out a well mannered cautioning and the explanation behind the slip utilizing mysql_error.

Introducing

PEAR utilizes a Package Manager that regulates which PEAR highlights you introduce. Whether you have to introduce the Package Manager relies on upon which form of PHP you introduced. If you're running PHP 4.3.0 or more up to date, it's now introduced. If you're running PHP 5.0, PEAR has been split out into a different bundle. The DB bundle that you're keen on is discretionary however introduced as a matter of course with the Package Manager. So if you have the Package Manager, you're good to go.

Unix

You can introduce the Package Manager on a Unix system by executing the accompanying from the shell (charge line) brief:

lynx - source http://go-pear.org/| php

This takes the output of the go-pear.org site (which is really the source PHP code) to introduce PEAR and passes it along to the php charge for execution.

Windows

The PHP 5 establishment incorporates the PEAR establishment script as C:\php\go-pear.bat. In case you didn't introduce every one of the documents in Chapter 2, thumbs up and remove all the PHP records to C:/php from the charge incite, and execute the .bat record. If you introduced PHP from the MSI installer, you may need to execute the accompanying rather than the go-pear.bat record:

php go-pear.phar

If the PEAR catalog does not exists at all you'll have to re-run the PHP MSI installer, select the Change alternative, and set Extensions and Additional items to "Will be introduced on nearby commute" before running go-pear.phar.

The PEAR installer makes a document called C:\php\PEAR_ENV.reg. You have to double-click to set up the PEAR ways in the registry. This document is dependent upon which PEAR form you introduced. At the point when the dialog seems to verify your data, you will add this to the registry and snap OK.

You may need to alter the php.ini document subsequent to running this .bat record to include the PEAR index to the incorporate way. Line 447 of php.ini now resembles this:

include_path = ".;c:\php\includes;c:\php\PEAR"

Apache must be restarted before the DB bundle can be utilized.

Facilitated ISP

Most ISPs have PEAR DB introduced. Request that your ISP introduce it if they haven't as of now. You can tell whether PEAR DB has been introduced by attempting the PHP code in Sample 9-8 to see whether the require_once ('DB.php'); line causes a mistake when the script is executed.

Including Additional Packages

Once that is finished, you can get to the PEAR Package Manager by entering pear at the summon brief. Including new modules is as simple as executing pear packagename.

Making an associate occasion

The DB.php record characterizes a class of sort DB. Allude to Chapter 5 for more data on meeting expectations with classes and objects. We'll basically be calling the strategies in the class. The DB class has a join technique, which we'll use rather than our old interface

function, mysql_connect. The twofold colons (::) show that we're calling that function from the class in line 4:

$connection = DB::connect("mysql://$db_username:$db_password@$db_host/$db_database");

When you call the join function, it makes another database association that is put away in the variable $connection. The join function endeavors to associate with the database taking into account the join string you went to it.

Associate string

The associate string uses this new arrangement to speak to the login data that you effectively supplied in isolated fields:

dbtype://username:password@host/database

This organization may look well known to you, as it's fundamentally the same to the unite string for a Windows record offer. The primary piece of the string is the thing that truly sets the PEAR functions separated from the plain PHP. The phptype field specifies the kind of database to join.

Bolstered databases incorporate ibase, msql, mssql, mysql, oci8, odbc, pgsql, and sybase. All that is needed for your PHP page to work with a different kind of database is changing the phptype!

The username, secret key, host, and database ought to be natural from the essential PHP interface. Just the sort of association is needed. Be that as it may, you'll typically need to specify all fields.

After the qualities from db_login.php are incorporated, the interface string resembles the taking after:

"mysql://test:test@localhost/test"

If the interface strategy on line 6 was fruitful, a DB object is made. It contains the routines to get to the database and the greater part of the data about the condition of that database association.

Questioning

One of the techniques it contains is called inquiry. The question strategy meets expectations simply like PHP's question function in that it takes a SQL statement.

CHAPTER 12

WORKING WITH FORMS

HTML structures give an approach to send significant information from the client to the server where it can be handled. You'll be utilizing a considerable measure of the PHP dialect ideas that you found out about in the first a large portion of the book to handle and approve the structure information.

We'll start by building a basic shape and figuring out how to get to the data in its fields after a client's accommodation. We'll examine the fundamental sorts of info gadgets that can be set on structures, and also on concealed qualities. Obviously, the PHP code will be blended in with these components.

Structures work in a two-stage process. The structure must be exhibited to the client. He then enters data and presents the structure. Each structure has an objective for what page to load that will transform the information when the client submits. Frequently, this is the same document that initially created the structure. The PHP code just verifies whether there's client data sticking the solicitation for the page to figure out if the document is being called to produce the structure or procedure its information.

Looking a database is fundamental in a wide range of sorts of utilizations. Whether it's looking discussion posts, clients, or a web journal, it can make a client's life much less demanding. On a database level, there are likewise a wide range of approaches to process an inquiry and bring back results.

12.1 Building a Form

Since you'll require a spot for the client to enter a pursuit question, we should start by building a structure to handle the client's information. Each structure must have these fundamental parts:

• The accommodation sort characterized with the strategy magic word

• One or more data components characterized with the information tag

• The destination to go to when submitted characterized with the activity magic word

We should manufacture a basic structure with a content information field called hunt and a submit catch, as indicated in Example 10-1.

Place the code in Example 10-1 into a document called simple.php in a web-available catalog on your web server, for example, the record root. Entirely talking, structures are characterized simply by HTML, yet we're utilizing some PHP code on line 6 to reference the "PHP_SELF" component of the earth variable array "$_SERVER". This gives aalternate route to the name of the current PHP document that handles the accommodation of the structure information.

The form in Example 10-1 permits you to catch the quest string from the client for a seek. Notice how we wrapped a name tag around the information where the content was; this makes the structure simpler to utilize. Tapping on the Search: message naturally sends the cursor to the hunt field. In line 6, we set the structure accommodation system to GET.

This is done to guarantee that clients can bookmark their ventures and not need to come back to the page and reappear their information. Line 8 does the greater part of the work by characterizing the content field.

Getting to the simple.php document from your program ought to create a formsimilar to Figure 10-1.
It's not awfully helpful, as any worth you submit just brings the same shape back once more, yet we'll deal with that.

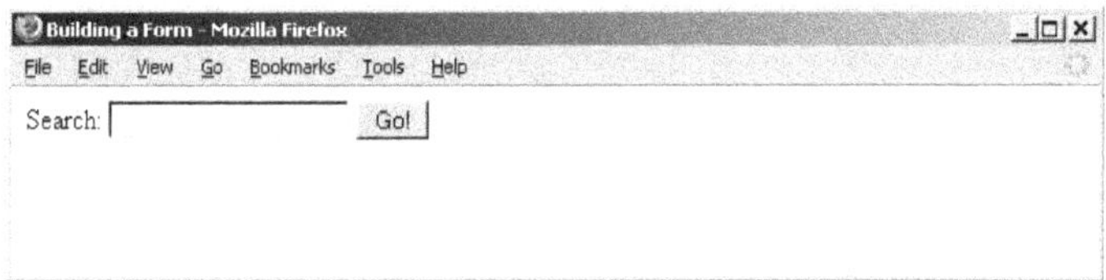

How the sample form appears in your browser

Default Values

At the point when performing quests on a database, you may need to really have some default values in your structures. This is valuable, for instance, for looking inside of a cost range. The client wouldn't generally like to embed qualities, and it makes it that much less difficult at the point when seeking. Ordinarily, the default esteem for a form element is situated with the worth property; on the other hand, there is a special case for checkboxes that utilization the checked catchphrase.

Types of Input

There are various sorts of data, so which one would it be a good idea for you to utilize? Radio catches, checkboxes, content, data, content territories, buttons...oh my! We'll portray each of our info choices.

- ✓ Text boxes

More often than not when managing info from a client, you may need a string of content. A content sort component is utilized to catch these strings from the client. The name credit is obliged to handle the info after a formsubm ission as it specifies how to reference the quality. When it shows up in the program, the size parameter decides the length of the content box. The maxlength parameter decides the most extreme number of characters the client can put in the field. The linguistic structure is as per the following:

<input type="text" name="name" size="display size" maxlength="max characters permitted"/>

✓ Checkboxes

A checkbox is helpful when you need to give clients a few different alternatives, particularly when they're permitted to choose every decision separately. Use checkboxes just when you have a couple of alternatives to provide for a client; generally, there is a different kind of data that you would need to utilize. This is known as a select, which we'll discuss in a bit. For a checkbox, set the information sort to checkbox. The name and worth properties are likewise needed. If the worth is situated to checked, the checkbox is checked as a matter of course.

Not at all like the earlier information sorts, has checkbox given back an array. Obviously, living up to expectations with different qualities will be talked about later in this part.

12.2 Templates

At whatever point you are taking information from a client, you ought to accept it. If you do not accept the client's information, it can bring about numerous issues—including conceivable security dangers.

Accepting data is not muddled. We'll go over the most widely recognized PHP functions that are utilized to disinfect information from clients. Accepting checkboxes, radio catches, and chooses Accepting information that originates from checkboxes; radio catches, and chooses is simpler than accepting free arrangement fields, for example, content boxes in light of the fact that the quality ought to just be one of the predefined qualities. To guarantee this, store the majority of the alternatives in an array, and verify the client info is a piece of the array when you prepare the information. We'll take a gander at the code for checking info from a single choice (at the end of the day, one and only checkbox, radio catch, or other determination).

Querying the Database with Form Data

Once you've approved your information, you're prepared to begin utilizing data from the structures in your database inquiries. Case 10-11 makes a function called query_db from the code in Chapter 7 for showing creators with a change to line 11 that permits coordinating the title with a LIKE inquiry condition. LIKE and NOT LIKE are for the most part utilized with strings and conceivably with special cases, for example, the underscore (_) and the percent sign (%).

- The underscore (_) matches a solitary character.
- The percent sign (%) matches zero or more characters.

In Example 10-10, the function takes a solitary parameter and hunt down the specific book title you're hoping to discover.

Sample 10.10. Consolidating structure handling and database questioning

```
<?php
function query_db($qstring) {
include('db_login.php');/association subtle elements
require_once('DB.php');/PEAR DB
$connection = DB::connect("mysql://$db_username:$db_password@$db_host/$db_ database");
if (DB::isError($connection)){/check for join mistakes
kick the bucket ("Could not interface with the database: <br/>". DB::
errorMessage($connection));
```

Formats

Formats isolate the HTML code that characterizes the presentation or look of a page from the PHP code that is in charge of social event the information. Once isolated, it gets to be less demanding for somebody with HTML and maybe CSS learning to modify the layout without agonizing over breaking the PHP code. Moreover, the PHP code can concentrate on the information as opposed to becoming involved with presentation subtle elements.

There are different points of interest to utilizing layouts, as well. If you commit an error in the layout, the slip will be plainly come back from the layout. The layout itself canfor the most part be stacked into a web program or a graphical web advancement instrument, for example, Dreamweaver, since it looks like the last condition of the page when handled. Layouts backing extremely essential programming elements for utilization with presentation, for example, having the capacity to tell whether an area of a page ought to be obvious.

Obviously, nothing's ideal; there are two or three drawbacks to layouts. Formats expand the quantity of records to keep up. They include a little measure of additional handling time. They likewise oblige introducing the layout motor and setting up registries. You should be running in any event PHP Version 4.0.6 to utilize Smarty, a famous format motor.

Format Engine

There are a few format bundles accessible on the Internet. Every uses its own layout motor to prepare the formats and make them as effective as could be expected under the circumstances. No matter which format motor you utilize, you'll generally take after the same fundamental steps:

1. Recover your information.

2. Make calls to the format functions for every quality that is utilized as a part of a layout.

3. Show the format utilizing the layout function.

We'll stroll through this procedure with a few samples in the blink of an eye. One of the more prominent layout motors accessible is Smarty, demonstrated later in Figure 10-16. Smarty has numerous, numerous elements; however we're most concerned with the fundamental layout motor functionality.

Establishment

While introducing Smarty isn't as mind boggling as introducing and designing Apache, PHP, what's more, MySQL, regardless it merits some consideration:

Application level indexes

For every application with which you wish to utilize Smarty, you'll have to set up a set of four indexes. The four indexes are for formats, assembled layouts, reserved layouts, and design records. In spite of the fact that you may not utilize those highlights, you ought to set up the indexes just on the off chance that you do:

1. Make an index called myapp/in your archive root. (You can call it whatever you need, yet for the rest of the content, we will allude to it as myapp/.)

2. Make a registry named smarty inside the catalog you simply made (myapp/ smarty).

3. In the smarty registry you simply made, make four more registries: formats,templates_c, store, and config. Guarantee that the web server will have compose access to the templates_c and store indexes that you

made in the past step.

You should only make a design and a PHP file to give it a try.

CHAPTER 13

PRACTICAL PHP

In this chapter we'll start trying of the more regular tasks that you'll perform when composing PHP programs, for example, working with strings, and showing different organizations for strings, dates, and times. We'll additionally demonstrate to you industry standards to work with documents that your PHP program creates or peruses. What's more, we'll give a case of how to let a client transfer a document and afterward accept its substance before making it open. Transferring documents is helpful yet can be a security hazard if records aren't legitimately accepted.

At the point when building HTML output for pages, we invest a considerable amount of energy working with strings. PHP has a rich arrangement of functions for doing every one of the assignments you may need to change the instance of a string. You likewise should have the capacity to arrangement dates and times. Performing any kind of expansion or subtraction on dates—on account of characteristics, for example, jump a long time—can rapidly get to be muddled without a little assistance from functions specifically intended to work with dates.

13.1 String Functions

Since you're working with essentially to languages that both help manipulating strings, you'll require knowledge about string functions in PHP and in MySQL. You might think that its more proper to modify a string either in a question or in PHP in view of the specific circumstance. You're going to find out about the accompanying string operations:

• Formatting strings for showcase

• Calculating the length of a string

• Changing a string's case to capitalized or lowercase

• Searching for strings inside of strings and giving back the position of the match

• Returning only a part of a string, which is a substring We'll begin with arranging strings, since that will help you all through whatever remains of the subjects.

Formatting Strings for Display

In this way, you've been utilizing echo and print to show strings without much modification.

You'll find out around two functions called printf and sprintf. If you're well known with other programming dialects, for example, C, you'll perceive that these functions work the same path as they do elsewhere. Try not to stress if you haven't utilized them before—they're not very difficult to work with. The main difference between the two is that printf shows an organized string to the output like print does, while sprintf spares the string it manufactures as another string with a name specified by you.

Using printf

The printf function lives up to expectations by taking as its first parameter an extraordinary designing string. The arranging string works like a format to depict how to plug whatever is left of the parameters into one subsequent string. You can specify subtle elements, for example, how to design numbers in the string or the cushioning of qualities. Every parameter that is set into the coming about string has a placeholder in the designing string. Case in point, to output a paired number.

Cushioning

You can likewise specify cushioning for every field. To left cushion a field with zeros, put a zero after the transformation specification percent sign (%) trailed by the quantity of zeros to cushion the sort specifier, as demonstrated in Example 11-4. If the output of the parameter employments less spaces than the number you specify, zeros are filled in on the left.

13.2 Date and time functions

Some of the times you'll need to change what number of digits shows up after a decimal point for a genuine (drifting point) number. This is particularly genuine if you have to print in money position. To specify the quantity of digits to use after the decimal point, utilize a change specifies that has a decimal point after the rate sign took after by the number of decimals. Case in point, the accompanying code demonstrates to you best practices to do it:

%.number_of_decimals_to_displayf

Document Manipulation

There may be times when you would prefer not to store data in a database and may need to work straightforwardly with a record. A case is a log file that tracks when your application can't join with the database. It is difficult to keep this data in the database in light of the fact that it's not accessible at precisely the time you'd require to keep in touch with it. PHP gives functions to record control that can perform the following:

- Check the presence of a record
- Create a record
- Append to a record
- Rename a record
- Delete a record

We've officially talked about the incorporate and oblige functions for pulling data specifically into a PHP script. At this crossroads, we'll concentrate on meeting expectations with document content.

Functions and Precautions

To check for the presence of a document, utilize the function file_exists, which takes the name of the document to check for its parameter, as demonstrated in Example 11-20. If the record exists, it returns TRUE; else, it returns FALSE.

As you would expect, the record does exist:

The record exists.php does exist.

PHP gives a few functions to let you know about different record properties. PHP has the capacity to peruse information from, and compose information to, records on your framework. On the other hand, it doesn't stop there. It accompanies a full-highlighted document and-catalog control API that permits you to:

- View and modify document characteristics
- Read and rundown catalog substance
- Alter document consents
- Retrieve document substance into an assortment of local information structures
- Search for documents in light of specific examples

The greater part of this document control through the API is hearty and adaptable. PHP has a considerable measure of extraordinary orders, including all the document control ones.

13.3 File Manipulation

Since you know a document exists, you may believe you're done, yet you're most certainly not. Just since the record is there doesn't mean you can read, compose, or execute it. To check for these properties, use is_readable to check for read access, is_writable to check for compose access, and is_executable to check for the capacity to execute the document. Every function takes a filename as its parameter. Unless you know the record is in the same catalog as your script, you must specify a full way to the record in the filename. You can use connecting to put the way and filename together, as in:

$file_name = $path_to_file . $file_name_only;

URL Wrappers

Two URL conventions that PHP has constructed in for utilization with the file system functions incorporate open and duplicate. Notwithstanding these two wrappers, as of PHP 4.3.0, you can compose your own particular wrappers utilizing a PHP script and stream_wrapper_register. The default wrapper is record://, utilized with PHP, and it is the nearby filesystem. If you specify a relative way, which is one that doesn't start with/, \, \\, or a Windows drive letter, for example, C://, the way gave applies against the present working index.

Generally this is the place the script lives, unless obviously it's been changed. With a few functions, for example, fopen and file_get_contents, include_path can be used to hunt down relative ways too.

13.4 Calling System Calls

It's a genuinely basic prerequisite for a PHP-based site to permit document transfers. For sample, on a web journal webpage, a client may need to transfer a picture to run with his post.

We'll stroll through the progressions to transfer a document on the grounds that you'll be planning a website in Section 17. PHP permits you to do this with the assistance of structures data.

When you utilize the document transfer form field, the customer's program pulls up a record choice dialog, so you don't need to stress over doing that. The code to incorporate in the document transfer field is <input type="file" name="file">. You should likewise include enctype= "multipart/structure" to the structure tag. This permits a document to be sent with the form submission.

CHAPTER 14

XHTML

Since you've taken in the establishments of utilizing PHP and MySQL to assemble dynamic pages, take sooner or later to investigate changes to the HTML markup that structures the premise of your website pages. You'll find out about XHTML, what it requests, and why it's worth the additional push to create. Keep in mind that so as to create quality web content from your PHP scripts, the markup must be benchmarks conformant. Consider the XHTML output as the completed item during the time spent asking for a page after PHP and a database functions process. We'll additionally examine approving the XHTML output that your scripts produce to get any mistakes.

XHTML remains for Extensible HyperText Markup Language. XHTML is a markup dialect that is like HTML, however with a stricter grammar, in light of the prerequisites of XML. HTML was based on SGML, which is adaptable yet complex to handle, also, XML stripped down SGML to make it simpler to transform if a touch less adaptable. XHTML linguistic structure looks much like HTML language structure, utilizing more prominent and not as much as signs (< furthermore, >) to characterize labels, yet has much stricter necessities for how those labels are conveyed. XHTML records that meet those syntactic necessities are called very much framed, while XHTML records that meet the linguistic structure in addition to the auxiliary principles contained in the DTDs are called substantial. XHTML reports can be handled naturally utilizing any standard XML library, while most HTML usage utilize a really merciful parser normally modified for HTML preparing. You can consider XHTML the crossing point of HTML and XML in numerous regards, since it's a reformulation of them two. Probably the simplest approach to exhibit what changes is to show a report in HTML and its XHTML equivalent. To begin with, here is a substantial HTML 4.0 report:

What's changed here?

• There's another XML declaration at the absolute beginning, identifying the report as XML 1.0, utilizing the UTF-8 character encoding. You can skirt this totally if your archive utilizes the UTF-8 encoding (or ASCII, which is a subset).

• The DOCTYPE presentation has changed marginally.

• All of the HTML markup is presently in lowercase. (The XHTML spec requires lowercase.)

• The html component now contains a xmlns property (characterizing the XHTML namespace, depicted later in this part), and in addition a xml:lang property that supplements the earlier lang quality for XML processors.

• The <BR> tag is presently a <br/> tag, with the cut (/) toward the end demonstrating that it's an "unfilled component" and won't have an end tag.

• There's another shutting tag, </p>, which finishes the <p> on the first line inside of the body. XHTML doesn't give you a chance to have a begin tag without an end tag unless you utilize the void component documentation utilized for <br/>. In spite of the fact that this record is too short to show a lot of it, the request of opening and shutting labels likewise needs to be symmetrical; <b><i>This is striking italic</i></b> is fine, however <b><i>This is striking italic</b></i> isn't right. This makes the archive structure unequivocal for any system that needs to handle or modify it.

As we'll see later, there are a couple of different confinements, yet these are the key things to look for.

14.1 Why XHTML?

The World Wide Web Consortium (W3C) made XHTML for various reasons, including the following:

• Web substance is conveyed to a larger number of gadgets than customary PCs, for example, Blackberries, phones, and other cell phones. XML's more tightly language structure evacuates one layer of complex handling for these gadgets and their backing framework to handle.

• Developers working with Dynamic HTML and other scripting innovations found that HTML's adaptability some of the time implied that the archive structures they expected to control looked somewhat different than anticipated, now and then indeed, even different from browser to program. XHTML's more tightly structures uproot these ambiguities.

• As more archive administration instruments included XML backing, XHTML's XML similarity made it simple to utilize these apparatuses on XHTML with no tweaking.

• On a wide scale, XHTML empowers more prominent consistency among reports. While XML's stricter mistake checking may sound like a weight, it makes it simple to spot and right mistakes.

• While it hasn't discovered much program bolster, the W3C was trusting that moving to a XML establishment would let designers make custom vocabularies for blending with the excellent HTML vocabulary. The W3C's own arrangements included deal with sight and sound, design, and structures.

• XHTML could likewise be blended into other XML vocabularies, making it simpler to reuse this broadly comprehended vocabulary in new settings.

XML's sudden notoriety drove a reevaluating of why and how HTML was utilized, at minimum inside of norms bodies. While different programs moved to bolster XML and XHTML to some degree, it's a long way from being an obliged piece of the web improvement toolbox. The W3C acknowledged the first form of XHTML on January 26, 2000. The excellence of XML is that it obliges programs to fizzle when experiencing erroneously made XML. This means a XHTML program can more often than not run all the more effortlessly furthermore, speedier on littler gadgets than on a tantamount HTML program. It moreover urges Web creators to deliver more steady records. While stricter lapse checking may sound like a weight, the proposal for programs to post an lapse as opposed to endeavor to render mistakenly shaped substance ought to dispose of the issue by driving creators to redress their errors.

14.2 XHTML and XML Namespaces

XML is fantastically nonexclusive. It characterizes punctuation and fundamental structure, however it doesn't specify much about inquiries, for example, what components and qualities ought to be named. Any individual who needs to make a XML vocabulary can do as such without needing to contact the W3C or another gauges body. This makes an issue: Title in one connection may mean something completely different than Title in a different connection. The Namespaces in XML specification (which can be found at http://www.w3.org/TR/ REC-xml-names/) gives a system that designers can use to identify specific vocabularies utilizing Uniform Resource Identifiers (URIs). URIs are a blend of the well known Uniform Resource Locators (URLs) and Uniform Asset Names (URNs). From the point of view of XML namespaces, URIs are helpful on the grounds that they join an effortlessly utilized grammar with a thought of possession. The W3C claims names that begin with http://www.w3.org/, so it bodes well for them to utilize those as identifiers. In plain-vanilla XHTML with no different vocabularies blended in, the namespace is announced on the html component utilizing the XHTML property xmlns. Case in point:

<html xmlns="http://www.w3.org/1999/xhtml" >

The namespace URI http://www.w3.org/1999/xhtml now applies to the html component itself and to any kid components, insofar as they don't have either their own particular xmlns traits or names that begin with a prefix and colon.

14.3 XHTML Versions

Since its beginning, the XHTML standard has been always advancing. There are three noteworthy forms being used today:

XHTML 1.0

XHTML 1.0 has the same contents as HTML 4.01, however it needs the use of XML syntax.

XHTML 1.1

XHTML 1.1 is a module-based reformatted form of the

1.0 discharge. It's strict since it utilizes an arrangement of modules that are chosen from a much bigger set characterized in the Modularization of XHTML. This is a W3C suggestion that gives a modularization structure, modules that have a standard set and various definitions that need to conform to the XHTML environment. Any deplored elements of HTML, for example, presentational components and framesets, have been expelled from this variant. All program based presentation is controlled by Cascading Templates ((CSS). Moreover, 1.1 includes Ruby markup bolster, which is required for East Asian dialects.

14.4 Creating XHTML with PHP

Producing XHTML from your PHP code is not any more difficult than making plain old HTML (see Example 14.4).

Illustration 14.4. Making a XHTML record from PHP

```
<?php

/Ask the program if it thinks about the application/
xthml+xml MIME sort

/This is necesary as a result of IE

if(stristr($_SERVER["HTTP_
ACCEPT"],"application/xhtml+xml")) {

header('Content-Type: application/xhtml+xml;
charset=utf-8');
```

```
}
else {
header('Content-Type: content/html; charset=utf-8');
}
/Create the archive sort
$doctype = '<?xml version="1.0"
encoding="UTF-8"?>';
$doctype .= '<!DOCTYPE html PUBLIC "-/W3C//
DTD XHTML 1.0 Strict//EN" ';
$doctype .= " "http://www.w3.org/TR/xhtml1/DTD/
xhtml1-strict.dtd"> ';
/Create the heading
$head= '<html xmlns="http://www.w3.org/1999/
xhtml" xml:lang="en" lang="en">';
$head .= " <head>';
$head .= " <title>Document Type Declaration Ex-
ample</title>';
$head .= " </head>';
/Create the body content
$body = " <body>';
$body .= " <p>The substance of the page goes here.</
p>';
```

```
$body .= " </body>';
/Create the footer content
$footer = '</html>';
/Display it all together
echo $doctype;
echo $head;
echo $body;
echo $footer;
?>
```

Because we've secured XHTML, which enhances standard HTML and the compatibility of your site, we're prepared to proceed onward to concepts that start to blend PHP and MySQL procedures together. In the following chapter, we'll discuss modifying database objects and information in MySQL from within PHP. We'll also learn how to make dynamic HTML joins that perform actions on specific data from the database.

CHAPTER 15

MODIFYING MYSQL OBJECTS AND PHP DATA

15.1 Changing Database Objects from PHP

The SQL inquiry string remains the basic apparatus for giving database commands. You can simply make and modify database objects with standard SQL that is called the same way you execute queries. Some of the time you'll need to make database objects from within PHP. We'll start with making a table, which is an example of making objects.

15.2 Manipulating Table Data

We've previously made the books and authors tables, but we haven't made the buyers table. We'll make one using the PHP shown as a part of Example 15.1.

Example 15.1. Making a table from a PHP page in create_table.php

```
<?php

include('db_login.php');

require_once( "DB.php" );

$connection = DB::connect( "mysql://$db_username:$db_password@$db_host/$db_database");
```

```
if (!$connection)
{
bite the dust ("Could not interface with the database: <br>". DB::errorMessage( ));
};
$query = 'Make TABLE buys (
purchase_id int(11) NOT NULL auto_increment,
```

Dropping a Table

Illustration 15.2 drops the table you created from the above code.

Illustration 15.2. Dropping the buyers table in drop.php

```
<?php
require_once('db_login.php');
require_once('DB.php');
$connection = DB::connect("mysql://$db_username:$db_password@$db_host/$db_database");
if (DB::isError($connection)){
pass on ("Could not associate with the database: <br/>". DB::errorMessage($connection));
}
$query = "DROP TABLE buys";
$result = $connection->query($query);
```

```
if (DB::isError($result)){
die("Could not inquiry the database: <br/>". $query."
".DB::errorMessage($result));
}
echo "Table dropped effectively!";
$connection->disconnect( );
?>
```

That worked incredibly, however you're going to require the buys table, so how about we reproduce the table by calling the create_table.php code in Example 13-1. Since you're modifying objects, there's a probability that the database won't give you a chance to do what you request that it do, which is the place lapses can happen. Dropping tables dangers information misfortune. Be extremely cautious about utilizing DROP!

Lapses Happen

To verify you handle a lapse legitimately such as a grammatical error in the CREATE statement then again, for this situation, attempting to make a table that as of now exists—execute the create_table. php script once more.

Expecting that your object was made without a lapse, you're going to need to control and add information to it from PHP. Hence, next you'll add information to a current table in light of information from the client.

15.3 Manipulating Table Data

Since you've worked on executing a couple SQL commands that control database objects, you're prepared to work with the data in your tables. You will be utilizing the same SQL commands as when you made them from the MySQL prompt, however, now we're going to coordinate client information inside PHP.

Adding Data

Actually, you'll have to add rows to your tables because that you're embedding new data.

To add a buy to your new buyers table, you'll use an INSERT statement in your query. Illustration 15.3 shows how this is done. Feel free to run example 15.1 again so you have a table in which to insert the information.

Example 13.3. Using a predefined INSERT statement as a part of insert.php

```
<?php

require_once(‘db_login.php’);

require_once(‘DB.php’);

$connection = DB::connect(“mysql://$db_username:$db_password@$db_host/$db_database”);

if (DB::isError($connection)){

bite the dust (“Could not associate with the database: <br/>”. DB::errorMessage($connection));

}
```

```
$query = "Embed INTO buys VALUES (NULL,'mdavis',2,NULL)";

$result = $connection->query($query);

if (DB::isError($result)){

die("Could not inquiry the database: <br/>". $query." ".DB::errorMessage($result));

}

echo "Embedded effectively!";

$connection->disconnect( );

?>
```

Displaying Results with Embedded Links

You may need to give your web browser the capacity to click a hyperlink to launch an activity that relates to the present row in the outcomes from a query. You do this by including URL links to the results of the query when they show on the screen. The links contain a distinctive identifier to the row and the script that handles the activity.

The PHP script that is the target of the link mainly queries the database in light of the distinctive identifier that was passed to it. The types of activity you can do range from formatting or erasing a row to developing details from a related table, for example, writers for book titles.

www.ingramcontent.com/pod-product-compliance
Lightning Source LLC
LaVergne TN
LVHW022306060326
832902LV00020B/3305

* 9 7 8 1 5 1 6 9 2 7 4 9 4 *